WORSHIP!

Making Primary School Collective Worship Come Alive

WORSHIP!

Making Primary School
Collective Worship Come Alive

John Bailey

Illustrations by Richard Warren

The National Society
A Christian Voice in Education

a co-publication with
Church House Publishing

Church House Publishing,
Church House,
Great Smith Street,
London SW1P 3NZ

ISBN 0 7151 4915 6

Published 1999 by Church House Publishing

Cover design by Leigh Hurlock

Printed by Biddles Ltd, Guildford and King's Lynn

Contents

List of Sources

Unless otherwise specified, the act of worship is intended for the whole primary age range (4–11).

All Bible stories included are versions written by the author.

Contributing Schools

Allington with Sedgebrook, Grantham

Allithwaite, Grange over Sands

Archdeacon Griffiths Primary, Llyswen, Brecon

Barnwood, Gloucester

Belton, North Lincs

Bishop Goodwin, Carlisle

Church Hill Junior, Thurmaston, Leicester

East Ravendale, North East Lincs

Lisle Marsden Infant, Grimsby

Littleton, Shepperton

Llangattock, Crickhowell

Long Bennington, Lincs

Malden Parochial, Worcester Park, Surrey

National Junior, Grantham

Newbridge at St John's, Bath

Rhayader Primary, Powys

St David's First, Exeter

St James and St Michael's, Paddington

St Martin's, Owston Ferry, North Lincs

St Mary's, Beverley

St Peter's, Droitwich

St Winnow, Lostwithiel, Cornwall

Winterton Infant, North Lincs

Acknowledgements

This book is dedicated to my wife, Susanne, without whose love and support I would have ground to a halt long ago; and to the staff of the Diocesan Education Centre in Lincoln, Paulette, Maurice, Linda, Margaret and Sally, whose unfailing cheerfulness and industry are a model of the caring communities we are seeking to celebrate in school worship.

I am particularly grateful to Sally Doughty for turning my manuscript into a legible typescript, and, to Richard Warren for the delightful illustrations, and to the many schools who so generously sent in ideas and suggestions.

The author and publisher gratefully acknowledge permission to reproduce copyright material in this publication. Every effort has been made to trace and contact copyright holders. If there are any inadvertent omissions we apologize to those concerned and will ensure that a suitable acknowledgement is made at the next reprint.

The Archbishops' Council: Extracts from *The Alternative Service Book 1980* are copyright © The Central Board of Finance of the Church of England 1980; The Archbishops' Council 1999 and are reproduced by permission (pp. 62, 97).

The Iona Community: Prayer from *A Wee Worship Book* is copyright © 1989 Wild Goose Worship Group, Iona Community, 840 Govan Road, Glasgow G57 3UU, Scotland (p. 37).

The Dean and Chapter of Lincoln Cathedral: Prayer for St Hugh from *Celebrating Common Prayer*, Mowbray, 1992 (p. 92).

National Society/Church House Publishing: Prayer of St Teresa of Avila from Christopher Herbert (compiler), *Pocket Prayers*, National Society/Church House Publishing, 1994 (p. 47).

John Bailey

Music book abbreviations

A	*Alleluyah!*, A & C Black, 1980
A & MR	*Hymns Ancient and Modern Revised*, Wm Clowes, 1972
BBP	*Big Blue Planet*, Stainer & Bell and Methodist Church Division of Education and Youth, 1995
CH	*The Complete Celebration Hymnal* (full music combined edition), McCrimmon Publishing Company, 1991
C & P	*Come & Praise*, BBC, 1990
CP	*Children's Praise*, Marshall Pickering, 1992
CT	*Chants Taizé*, HarperCollins, 1982
HON	*Hymns Old and New: New Anglican Edition*, Kevin Mayhew, 1996
JP	*Junior Praise* (combined music edition), Marshall Pickering, 1986
LA	John L. Bell and Graham Maule, *Love and Anger*, Wild Goose Publishing, 1997
LP	*Let's Praise*, Marshall Pickering, 1988
MP	*Mission Praise*, Marshall Pickering, 1992
MT	*Music from Taizé*, Vols 1 & 2, HarperCollins, 1982/85
MWS	*Make Way Songbook*, Kingsway, 1988
S	*The Source*, Kevin Mayhew, 1998
SoF	*Songs of Fellowship*, Kingsway, 1991
SoP	*Songs of Praise*, OUP, 1931
SSL	*Someone's Singing Lord*, A & C Black, 1973
TYM	Thank You Music
WP	*World Praise* (music edition), HarperCollins, 1993

Introduction

COLLECTIVE WORSHIP IN SCHOOLS

Collective worship in schools has been the subject of controversy in recent years, not least because the relentless eye of the OFSTED inspector has discovered many schools, particularly but not exclusively secondary schools, that are not complying with the daily requirement for collective worship. There have been many calls, from teachers' associations and others, for the 'daily' requirement to be relaxed; the requirement in Schedule 20 of the School Standards and Framework Act 1998, that in community schools, and foundation schools without a religious character, collective worship should be 'wholly or mainly of a broadly Christian character', has also been challenged as inappropriate in our multi-faith, multicultural society.

The debate rumbles on, and no doubt will continue to do so for many years to come. Certainly there is little sign of an imminent change in the law in respect of daily collective worship. What should be our response? How can Heads, governors, clergy, teachers and others who plan and lead collective worship in schools hold together these apparently irreconcilable views about school worship?

Let us concentrate first on the 'daily' aspect. There is strong evidence, particularly in primary schools, that bringing together the whole school or a significant part of the school (e.g. a key stage) on a daily basis is a powerful way of binding the community together, particularly if these occasions are used to celebrate and reinforce the values which that community holds dear. (Since the Latin word 'religio', bond, is the root of our word 'religion', we could even argue that

the simple act of coming together on a regular basis in this way is in itself religious!)

Secondly, we need to think about what goes on during these times of 'coming together'. Worship is a voluntary activity; the believer meets with other believers to worship, praise and adore the God in whom they all believe. Schools, whether community, foundation or voluntary, are not believing communities in that sense; they are collectives, in which children and adults with a variety of religious beliefs (and no beliefs at all!) come together. Hence, 'collective' worship, which is going to be a very different animal from the corporate worship of a body of believers in a church, mosque or synagogue.

BROADLY CHRISTIAN?

The wording of the School Standards and Framework Act 1998 (Schedule 20) in respect of collective worship in community schools, that it should be 'wholly or mainly of a broadly Christian character', is in fact an extremely flexible definition which allows for a wide range of interpretations, and one which we should not seek to abandon lightly. Most schools include in their aims something about learning to care for others; many refer to the building of a caring, loving society which values individuals; some speak of fostering reflection, awe and wonder. Could not these aims be said to be 'of a broadly Christian character'? And should we not be celebrating them, and seeking to reinforce them on a regular – perhaps daily – basis? And if so, isn't this what we mean by 'collective' worship?

In voluntary schools or foundation schools with a religious character, worship has to be in accordance with the school's Trust Deed (School Standards and Framework Act 1998,

Schedule 20 (5)). This may, of course, not be very helpful – some Trust Deeds simply say that 'St Ethelburga's was founded in 1853 for the education of the poor of the parish', and do not mention worship at all. It is for the governors of a church school to determine the policy for collective worship, and in the absence of clear guidance from a Trust Deed, they have to fall back on the Christian nature of the school's foundation, while at the same time being sensitive to the family backgrounds of the children in the school and the nature of the local community.

Whether they are community, foundation or voluntary, then, schools should be seeking to provide, on a daily basis, acts of collective worship which are of high quality, relevant to the needs and aspirations of the children (and adults!) present, take account of the faith backgrounds of the children as well as the legal requirement to keep within a 'broadly Christian' framework, and celebrate the shared values of the school. A tall order! But not one that we can shirk – indeed, according to OFSTED evidence, in primary schools at least, this is a task which most schools are facing up to very well.

One of the biggest challenges is preparation and planning. Fortunately, the days when the Head could be seen walking along the corridor to the assembly, flicking over the pages of a well-thumbed, 1940s book of assembly stories are long gone. Nowadays, most schools plan as carefully for their acts of collective worship as for any other aspect of the curriculum. This book is intended to be a contribution to that process.

QUALITY OF WORSHIP

What makes a 'good' act of collective worship in a primary school? First, it has to be worship! This doesn't necessarily mean it has to have prayers, hymns and Bible stories, although these may well be ingredients of successful worship. It does mean that the children should be focusing on important issues and concepts, such as love, forgive-

ness, caring for others; it certainly requires that there should be time for reflection and prayer; there must be a feeling that this time is somehow special, out of the ordinary, different; there must be an opportunity for spiritual development; and above all, while no one can force anyone else to worship, the act of collective worship should bring children to what John Hull has called 'the threshold of worship', so that those present who wish to and are able to, may cross that threshold and worship, in their own hearts and minds, the God in whom they believe.

Secondly, there should be plenty of participation– both active and passive – by all present, including adults. This means that, when appropriate, the children should be involved in leading the worship; the adults present should take part fully, not just supervise; all should be encouraged to take part in singing and saying prayers.

Thirdly, there should be plenty of variety of format: dramatic readings, stories, music, dance, mime, formal prayers, hymns and songs all have their place, over a period of days or weeks.

Fourthly, there should be a variety of leaders of worship. Of course the Head and senior teachers will be key figures in leading worship, but the children should expect visitors from outside the school to come in and speak at, or lead, collective worship: not just clergy and ministers, but leaders of other faiths, representatives of charitable organizations, local leaders and politicians, and 'ordinary' people from local churches and caring professions.

Fifthly, we must bear in mind the 'broadly Christian' requirement referred to above. This must mean, at the very least, that stories of, and told by, Jesus will be read, dramatized or performed; other Bible stories will be told and related to the theme of the worship; Christian hymns and prayers will be used, albeit not necessarily every day; and, particularly in church schools, the 'Red Letter Days' of the Christian calendar will be celebrated.

Finally, bearing in mind the religious and cultural mix of Britain today, we should expect to find some references to festivals of faiths other than Christian at appropriate times – even in schools with few, or no, adherents of other faiths.

HOW THIS BOOK CAME ABOUT

In many ways, this book is inspired by, and follows on from, *Key Stages: Developing Primary School Collective Worship* by Jackie Hughes and Yvonne Collins (National Society/Church House Publishing, 1996). It follows the same philosophy and understanding of collective worship, and fleshes out the cycles of themes given in *Key Stages* by offering over 70 individual acts of worship on many of those themes.

This is not, however, another collection of what used to be called 'school assemblies', although it does include a wide range of examples of good practice drawn from primary schools all over the country. Instead, a variety of different approaches to collective worship are explored, including ways of getting lots of children involved; how to write and produce scripted drama, and how to improvise drama; making Bible stories come alive, and in particular, re-enacting the life of Jesus; ways of using poetry and children's written work; writing and telling stories; using

music and dance; making use of visitors; developing a theme over a week; and using artefacts of various kinds.

Each of these approaches is illustrated by several examples of acts of worship which have been selected from a large number of primary schools from all over the country. The author wrote to the Diocesan Directors of Education in England and Wales, asking for names of primary schools identified by OFSTED and Section 23 reports as presenting good practice in collective worship. Letters were then sent to the Heads of these schools, inviting them to submit some original examples of acts of worship which had, in their view, been successful. The examples here are drawn from that pool. They have, of course, been edited, and to some extent developed, by the author, but the original ideas are from the schools.

Although the examples given are drawn from Church of England schools, they have been selected as being appropriate for county (community) schools as well. Some readily lend themselves to being reproduced as they stand in another school; others will need modifying to suit local circumstances; some (for example the acts of worship in the chapter on using visitors) are meant as examples to stimulate thinking about the range of visitors that might be invited and how they might be used.

1 Plenty of participation!

The most memorable and effective acts of collective worship, from the point of view of the children, are the ones in which they are involved. It follows that the more children you can involve in the worship (within reason), the better it will be. Of course there are many ways of involving the children; some of these, such as liturgy, drama, children's written work and dialogue, are exemplified in other chapters. The examples given in this chapter are notable because of the simple ways in which they involve children, without too much preparation.

Before we get to the examples, however, a word of caution. Remember that what we are about is worship. Not a music festival or a choral speaking competition, and not (unless it's a big end-of-term event) a costume drama, but worship. The spotlight, metaphorically speaking, is not on the performers but on the object of our worship: God, our Lord, the Creator, the Saviour, the ground of our being. The purpose of the participation is not 'look at me' but 'look at him' – and it is only effective as worship if we bear that in mind and if the children themselves are aware, however dimly, that this is what they are involved in.

Five examples follow, in which children hold up cards, read out words or sentences, come out to the front to write something on a whiteboard, read Bible stories, say their own prayers, tap out rhythms, show drawings and models they have made and, of course, answer questions, reflect quietly and sing hymns. The role of the leader of worship is still very important, to set the tone, keep things on course and keep an appropriate balance between excited anticipation and reflective worship. But however good we are as teachers and leaders of worship, occasions like these will succeed, and be remembered, because the children themselves are participating in leading the worship.

1.1 SUMMERTIME

Plenty of opportunities here to get the less able, less confident pupils taking part: the ones who don't usually shine as actors, singers or performers. Here they can hold up cards, say the word on the card, tap out rhythms and say in their own words what they saw coming to school. It's worship – not just because it includes hymns and prayers, but because it celebrates the beauty of the world in summer, the world that God gave us.

Age range: Key Stage 1

Candle to be lit while the children walk in quietly to music playing: Vivaldi, The Four Seasons – Summer.

Song: 'The Golden Cockerel' (SSL 2)

Leader: We are going to think about the seasons of the year.

Child 1: Holds up card 'Autumn', says word loudly, quieter, quieter.

Two children depict leaves falling down.

Repeat word and actions – whole school copies actions only.

Child 2: Holds up card 'Winter', says word loudly, quieter, quieter.

Two children stand by shivering.

Repeat word and actions – whole school copies actions only.

Child 3: Holds up card 'Spring', says word loudly, quieter, quieter.

Two children stand by clapping.

Repeat word and actions – whole school copies actions only.

Child 4: Holds up card 'Summer', says word quietly, louder, louder; then says 'Hip hip hip Hurray'.

Two children stand by moving arms in a swimming action.

Repeat word and actions using arms.

Everyone joins in 'Hip hip hip Hurray'.

Child 5: Everyone close your eyes and listen.

Quiet music to bring back quiet mood (short piece).

Prayer

God's world by day is full of light

He made the sun, so brilliantly bright

He set the moon to shine at night

God loved what he had done. Amen.

Rhythm game

I spied with my little eye on the way to school.

Tap out rhythm on knees and chant sentence (whole school).

Child 1: Reads out brief observation of what they saw coming to school.

Chant and tap rhythm.

Child 2: Reads out brief observation of what they saw coming to school.

Chant and tap rhythm.

Child 3: Reads out brief observation of what they saw coming to school.

Choir piece: Any suitable song on theme of summer, e.g. 'Thank you for the summer morning' (C & P 109).

Prayer

So praise the Lord – clap hands and
   sing.
Let's shout our praise for everything.
Let all the world with voices ring.
We love what God has done. Amen.

Rhythm game (contd)

Chant and tap rhythm (whole school).

Child 4: Reads out brief observation of what they saw coming to school.

Chant and tap rhythm.

Child 5: Reads out brief observation of what they saw coming to school.

Chant and tap rhythm.

Child 6: Reads out brief observation of what they saw coming to school.

Prayer

Dear Lord, you made this world so fair
With warm sunlight and fine fresh air.
May people praise you everywhere
For all that you have done. Amen.

The Lord's Prayer

Song: 'Colours of day' (C & P 55)

The Grace *(followed by candle being extinguished).*

1.2 THANK YOU!

Another opportunity for children to hold up cards; this time with a single letter per card, the whole spelling out different words depending on the order. This will require a bit of rehearsal! Plenty of opportunity for other children to come up and write the things they are thankful for. 'Thank you, Lord': the starting point for worship.

Resources Eight cards with the letters T.H.A.N.K.Y.O.U.

The beginning of this worship relies on the eight children having practised getting themselves into the 'right' positions. The leader can start by saying they would like to talk today about two special words and explain a bit more about them.

Children 1–8: Line up with cards which spell out 'AUNTY HOK'!

Leader: No, that's not right.

Children 1–8: Shuffle, 'HANKY OUT'!

Leader: No, that's not right either! Can anybody tell us what we really want to say? That's right. We want to say 'THANK YOU'.

The words can then form an acrostic for the things to be grateful for. If it is part of a class assembly, children can stand and say them in order, or write them on pieces of card and stick them somewhere as they are saying them, e.g. on whiteboards. If it is teacher-led, then volunteers can be asked to hold up cards. It can then be explained that these were just a few of the things we could say thank you for.

Leader: Some are things (*children stand/ stick things they are grateful for*).

Some are places (*children stand/stick names of places they are grateful for*).

Some are people (*children stand/stick names of people they are grateful for*).

So we know that we have lots of things to be very pleased with, and we have most of these things all week, so sometimes it is nice to stop and just say 'thank you'.

Being grateful and wanting to say 'thank you' is one thing. Doing it is another. When Jesus was on the earth, he did many things that people were grateful for. He gave them food. He calmed the storms. He helped people out of difficult situations and he told lots of people how much God loved them. One of the things he did most often was to make ill people better. There is a story about how one day he made ten people better at once.

The story of Jesus and the Ten Lepers can then be told: Luke 17.11-19.

Leader: All ten were healed; all ten were overjoyed; only one of them actually bothered to say 'thank you'. If you had been one of the ten, would you have gone back? (*Pause for thought*)

It is true that we have lots of things to be grateful for, and for a lot of them we would be like the nine who didn't say 'thank you' rather than the one who did. Think about all the people just in school whom we could say 'thank you' to for all the things they do for us.

All the support staff of the school with whom the children come into contact can then be highlighted: kitchen staff, premises officer, ancillaries, etc.

Leader: These are just the people in the school! When did you last say 'thank you' to any of these? (*Pause for thought*)

The leader may suggest that cards are made for these people, and left somewhere for all pupils to sign. These can then be presented in a later assembly.

Leader: One of the best ways to show you are thankful is to give. Sometimes it's right to give money or gifts. Sometimes all it takes is a word or a smile. The important thing is to do it because you think it's right, not because everyone will think you're great. If you give, don't shout about it, just do it!

Song: 'I come like a beggar' (C & P 90)

1.3 FRIENDSHIP

Another example using pre-prepared cards, this time ten of them: five saying nasty things we shouldn't do, five saying nice things. Ideally, these would be suggested by children in class beforehand and written out by them on the cards.

The act of worship involves the children who come out and hold up the cards; the rest of the children in deciding how to divide up the cards into two groups (not difficult, but it can be good fun); a Bible story, told by the teacher in his/her own words; a prayer, which includes words addressed to Jesus and an opportunity to reflect; and an appropriate hymn.

Cautionary note: The Bible story about Martha and Mary (in Luke chapter 10) could be taken as meaning that it is better to sit idly by and let someone else do all the work. It might be a good idea to pre-empt this possible interpretation when you tell the story in your own words, perhaps by emphasizing that both preparing the food and listening to Jesus are important. (A version of this story is given in 5.3.)

Preparation Prepare ten cards – five cards with nice things we do with friends, e.g. we should share our toys and games; and five cards with not so nice things, e.g. we should not say unkind words to each other.

Story/Role play

Tell or act out the story of Mary and Martha at Bethany (Luke 10. 38-42). Jesus told us that people are more important than a meal or belongings.

Discussion

Tell the children that you have ten sentences. Read the sentences together with the children, and hand each sentence to a child to hold up at the front of the assembly. Divide sentences into two groups – how we should behave/treat our friends and how we shouldn't treat our friends. How have you helped or shown kindness to a friend today?

Prayer

Jesus, thank you for our friends, for their love and laughter.

When you were on earth you had close friends like Mary and Martha.

Please look after my friends and help me to be a good friend. Amen.

Ask the children to keep their eyes closed, and to think of something kind they could do for a friend today.

Song: 'Bind us together Lord' (JP 17)

1.4 BABY AMRIK COMES TO SCHOOL (VISITORS)

When this was first performed, the characters really were Leela, her mother, and her baby brother Amrik.

Leela's mother wrote afterwards:

> The collective worship was very moving, and made Leela, Amrik and myself feel part of an extended family. It was an important occasion for Leela – she got a sense of achievement by being able to share a special event in her life with the school. It was hard to believe that a year ago Leela was so reluctant to attend school, and now she confidently stood in front of the school children to introduce her family.

The potential contribution to personal and social development provided by taking part in collective worship in this way is very evident.

You may be able to ask a 'mum' to bring her baby into school, in which case the name will be different. Or you may get children to play the parts of Leela and her mother and use a doll for baby Amrik.

Resources Candle, prepared gifts, prayers written beforehand by children.

A candle is lit. Children walk in to pan pipe music.

Reading

1 Timothy 4.10 (*child to read*).

Leader: Introduction in his/her own words, along these lines: A new baby, Amrik, is born. Leela is to introduce her mother and brother to the school. One day baby Amrik will grow up. What do we hope for him? What gift could we give him, so that he will have a good life?

The leader explains that five children have prepared what they would like to give to the baby.

Quiet music is played. One child from each class takes it in turn to walk to the baby. The music stops and the child touches the baby and gives the message: I give Hope – I give Happiness – I give the gift of Love, Friendship and Life.

Prayer

Children's own silent hopes and prayers for Amrik.

'Two little eyes' (JP 262) said as a prayer.

Going-out music: pan pipes. The children file out, past baby Amrik.

1.5 HOMES

This act of worship is part of an extended theme on 'Places' which could last anything from a week to half a term.

Aim: The objectives of the theme and the act of worship are:

● To develop the children's knowledge and awareness of themselves and their place in society.

● To invite children to share their thoughts and feelings about places which are important to them.

● To share our knowledge and understanding about places of worship.

Resources Could include: model of a house, picture of a house; simple drawing done for or by the children.

Issues raised with children through discussion in class, groups in class or whole school during assembly:

● The need to feel safe and secure.

● The need for warmth and comfort.

● The need to be with our loved ones (our families, friends and pets!).

● The need for privacy and freedom.

● The need to share a space with our loved ones and share activities, including meal times.

The participation by children during the worship includes holding up their pictures or models of a home; reading their own poems about the joys and problems of sharing a bedroom with a sibling (two examples are given); discussing with the leader what Jesus' home might have been like; songs and meditative prayer.

Music on entry: 'Back home again' by John Denver, or *New World* Symphony (Dvorak).

Initial discussion

Why do we need a home? Children may be invited to give responses or have previously prepared comments.

Main item

Our homes. A group of children to show their own representations of the home they live in (a very simplified version for young children to recognize immediately).

Poems

'I share my bedroom' by Michael Rosen, from *The Song that Sings the Bird*, edited by Ruth Craft (Harper-Collins, 1992). This is an excellent poem to spark children off in writing about their own shared bedrooms.

Here are two examples, written by children:

I Share My Bedroom

I share my bedroom with a little pest.
She snaps my planes and jumps on
    my bed.
Then again her friends call her back.
Whatever whatever whatever next.

David

David, David, the little pest.
David, David, not the best
Of brothers that are on this earth.
When my mummy gave him birth
He looked exactly like a Smurf!
I beamed with joy (Oh me! Oh my!)
OK then, I suppose it was a lie.
David's a great brother, you heard
    what I said,
Even if he beats me up in bed!

Leader reminds children of the type of home that Jesus shared with his family; the place where it was and the security and love it offered to the growing boy.

Prayer

Use prayers from Christopher Herbert, *Pocket Prayers for Children* (NS/CHP, 1999). Alternatively, children's own prayers could be read by them.

Song: 'The building song' (C & P 61), or 'He made me' (C & P 18)

Meditation

Moment of stillness and quiet thoughts on issues raised – a particular thought may be dwelt upon here.

Going-out music: 'Back home again' by John Denver, or New World Symphony (Dvorak).

1.6 PEACE

This is a very simple act of worship which involves everyone present in 'passing the Peace'. One child starts, by shaking hands with another child and saying, 'Peace be with you.' These two then pass the Peace on in the same way, and in the words of a teacher who wrote an evaluation of this act of worship, 'the sign of peace rippled out-ward like the ripples on a pond when a stone is dropped into it'.

This act of worship was first used on International Peace Day (20 September) but could be used on other occasions, or as part of another act of worship.

Introductory music: 'Last night I had the strangest dream' (BBC Records, REC 58M).

Song: 'Give me oil in my lamp' (C & P 43)

Leader:　Last Saturday (*or whenever*) was a special day. It was International Peace Day. This was a time for everyone to think about peace.

This has been a terrible century for wars. There have been two great World Wars in which many millions of men and women have been killed. We learn about these wars in our history lessons; but mankind never seems to learn the lesson properly, because wars keep on happening.

Perhaps you and I can't do much about wars between nations, but we can make a start by thinking about our own lives, and the little 'wars' that we sometimes have with other boys and girls, the squabbles and disagreements.

We're going to close our eyes for a moment and think about times in our lives when we have fallen out with someone, perhaps someone in our own class at school. (*Short period of silence*)

Now we're going to pass the Peace. I'm going to ask _____ to start (*pick a child in the middle of the hall*) and I'd like you to pass the Peace on to someone near you. It might be someone you have fallen out with, or said a cross word to, so that when you say, 'Peace be with you', you really mean it.

The Peace ripples out from the centre – see introduction.

Prayer

School Prayer, or other suitable prayer for peace.

Hymn: 'Light up the fire' (C & P 55)

2 Making up scripted drama

Most schools put on school plays or musicals from time to time. Sometimes these have a religious theme; *Joseph and the Amazing Technicolour Dreamcoat, Jonah Man Jazz, Captain Noah and His Floating Zoo*, for example. These may verge on worship, but they are written, and performed, primarily for entertainment. The purpose of this chapter is to look at ways in which drama can be written and performed as worship. These examples are not meant to be fantastic, amazing, creative acts of theatre that rival Shakespeare or Samuel Beckett in their profundity (although they are rather good!).

That would only serve to make you, the reader, despair and think that dramatic script-writing is best left to the experts. No, these are ordinary teachers, writing on ordinary everyday worship themes – Autumn/Harvest, Christmas, Peace, Easter. If you like them, perform them as they stand or with your own modifications or additions. But better still, have a go at writing your own scripts or dramatic presentations. 'Oh that's all very well for you to say,' I hear you snort. Okay, here's a tip. Often, stories in books, even in books of assembly material, have lots of dialogue and are just crying out to be turned into drama – leave out the 'he said' and 'she said', put the name of the person speaking in the margin, and Bob's your uncle – instant scripted drama. If you don't believe me, have a look at the story of the Passover in 9.3.

Even simpler – take a story and break it up into sections, with a different reader for each section, and add 'actors' who mime the actions that the readers are reading. The story of Handel (11.4) works like this; compare this version with the original in *Themework* (Stainer & Bell). This is so simple that the actors hardly need any rehearsal – although in that case, the results can sometimes be rather unpredictable . . .

2.1 AUTUMN/HARVEST SERVICE

This could be performed as it stands, as one special service, or broken down into component parts: Autumn; Canada; West Indies; Great Britain; Israel; Wales – St Cadoc and performed as separate but related acts of worship on successive days.

The hymns, songs, prayers, readings and dramatic interludes are skilfully interwoven to hold the interest and deepen our understanding of the meaning of Harvest Festival.

Candle to be lit at the start.

Hymn: 'Jubilate Deo' (SoF 315) (during which the harvest gifts are presented).

Poem

Autumn (*spoken by children*)
Yellow the bracken,
Golden the sheaves,
Rosy the apples,
Crimson the leaves;
Mist on the hillside,
Clouds, grey and white.
Autumn, good morning! (*whole class says 'good morning'*)
Summer, good night! (*whole class says 'good night'*)

Prayer

Spoken by children

Teach us, O God, that harvests are for sharing and that the good food you give should give life to all people. Help us to be thoughtful of the needs of others and not waste those things we have. Amen.

Hymn: 'Praise Him' (JP 203)

Reading

Children: Autumn is important, because it is the time when farmers gather in the crops which have been growing during the spring and summer. It is the time of year when the hedgerows are full of berries and when apples, plums and pears are hanging in the trees. It is the time for Harvest Festival services in churches everywhere, when people gather to say 'Thank you, God' for all the gifts of nature.

Come with us on a journey around the world and listen to the stories of harvests in different countries.

Song: 'He's got the whole world in his hands' (C & P 19)

Readers follow the banner of the country to the front.

Canada

Reader 1: Many years ago people went to Canada to make new homes for themselves and their families. Small groups of people found places where they could build their homes. They cut down trees and cleared land so that they could grow food to eat.

Reader 2: In one of these settlements, named Moose Creek, there was one store where people could buy things they needed. They often used to stop there to talk to each other because their farms were far

apart. They even used it as a church because there was no church building in Moose Creek. Then one day:

Old Jack: We ought to have a church. We have done very well since we came here five years ago.

Small group: Yes, yes, what a great idea.

Spokesman: Building a church would be one way of saying 'thank you' to God.

Reader 1: Sam was one of these men. As he rode home, he was thinking about the church. Then he said to himself:

Sam: I have huge fields of wheat growing around my cabin. God has been very good to me. I will give a quarter of my crop for the new church. Perhaps the money would pay for some lovely coloured windows to make the church beautiful.

Reader 2: So Sam worked hard and harvested the wheat. A few weeks later he set off with a wagon loaded with grain to travel the 30 miles to Moose Creek. He was thinking about the church and the windows when suddenly his horses refused to go any further.

Sam: Come on. Wait, I can smell burning.

Reader 1: As Sam looked ahead, he could see smoke rising from blackened fields. Leaving his wagon he rode over to the sad-looking people who stood nearby.

Group of people: It was all we had. We had spent all our money last year to buy the grain, now our harvest has gone. We have no money to buy food or any more grain.

Sam: I'll be back.

Reader 2: Sam thought about the church and the windows as he rode back to the wagon. He had made up his

mind. Soon he was back with his wagon of grain.

A farmer: We can't afford to buy that.

Sam: I'm not asking you to buy it. I'm giving it to you. I was going to buy windows for a church in Moose Creek but I'm sure this is a better way to say 'thank you' to God.

Prayer

Said by children

Teach us, O God, to share the good things we have and so bring happiness to other folk. Amen.

Hymn: 'Now we sing a harvest song' (C & P 138)

Readers follow the banner of the country to the front.

West Indies

Reader: On many of the islands of the West Indies the people enjoy special Harvest Sunday services. On the day before, they make their way to the church with all sorts of interesting fruits, nuts and roots. There are mangoes, melons, yams, peppers, sweet potatoes, bread, fruit and lots of other things as well. Some people travel long distances along uneven roads, carrying their produce in buckets on their heads or slung across the backs of their animals.

Readers follow the banner of the country to the middle.

Great Britain

Reader: Robert and Sarah come from a Christian home. Their parents attend the church near their home and the children go to the Sunday school. Each year at the beginning of October they have a special Harvest Festival Sunday, when the church is decorated with flowers, fruit and vegetables. They sing hymns about harvest time and thank God for all the good food and lovely flowers.

Poem

Read by children

Now all the farmers from far and wide
Have gathered their bounty of countryside:
Corn and barley from field and wold,
Honey from beehive and wool from the fold,
Fruit from the orchard all ripe, red and gold,
Log for the fire to keep out the cold.

Hymn: 'Think of a world' (C & P 17)

Readers follow the banner of the country to the middle.

Israel

Reader: Rachel belongs to a Jewish family. For eight days in the autumn her family have their meals in the garden under a shelter or booth. This is the festival of Sukkoth and it

has been kept by Jewish people for nearly 4,000 years. It is one of the festivals when Jewish people say 'thank you' for the harvest. They hold a special service in the synagogue and say 'thank you' for the grape harvest.

A long, long time ago, Moses had told people that when they had gathered their harvest, they were to put some of it into a basket and take it to the priest to be offered to God. This would be a way to say 'thank you' to God for a good harvest but also for God's goodness in giving them the Promised Land.

Prayer

Said by children

We thank thee then, O Father
For all things bright and good,
The seed time and the harvest,
Our life . . . our health . . . our food.
     (*Pause*)

Readers follow the banner of the country to the front.

Wales – St Cadoc

Reader 1: Long ago in the mountains of Wales there lived a boy named Cadoc. He loved God and wanted others to know him too. So he went to a village in the valley to learn from a holy man how he could teach them. He found that the people of the village were very sad. Bad weather had meant a bad harvest.

Cadoc: Ga'i aros a dysgu fod yn athro?

Reader 2: 'Can I stay and learn to be a teacher?' asked Cadoc. The holy man shook his head.

Holy man: Na, mae'n flin gen i does dim digon o fwyd i ti.

Reader 2: 'No, sorry, there is not enough food for you,' said the holy man. All the people of the village were praying to God for help so that they would not starve during the winter time.

Reader 1: Cadoc was disappointed. He went away and sat under a tree to think what he could do next. Then he heard a rustling sound. A little mouse had come out of a hole carrying a grain of wheat in its mouth. Soon it came back without the wheat, went into the hole and came out again with another grain of wheat. This happened again and again and again.

Cadoc: O ble mae'r llygoden yn cael y grawn?

Reader 2: 'Where is the mouse getting all the grain?' said Cadoc. He went to the village and returned with a group of men who had spades. They dug into the hillside and there, to everyone's surprise, they found a cellar which had once been part of an old house. The house had fallen into ruins long before and earth had covered the cellar. There in the old cellar were sacks of wheat – enough to feed

the people through the winter and leave some to sow in the fields in the spring.

Reader 1: So Cadoc was able to stay in the village and learn from the holy man. Then he returned to his mountains where people loved him and learned to love God too. Cadoc was such a good man that he became known as Saint Cadoc.

Hymn: 'Lord of the harvest' (C & P 133)

Blessing

Hymn: 'All things bright and beautiful' (C & P 3)

Candle to be extinguished.

2.2 THE LITTLE STAR: A PLAY FOR CHRISTMAS

Plenty of parts here, and opportunities for humour, foreign accents, audience participation and, finally, a Christmas message. Does this stand on its own, as an act of worship – or does it need hymns, carols, prayers? You decide.

Narrator: A number of stars are gathered in the heavens to talk about who will be chosen to mark the coming of

the king of kings, as revealed by an angel.

A row of children in costume stand across the stage.

Enter child in soldier's kit, pushing his/her way in.

Lucy/Luke: Out of my way.

I'm going to be the chosen star. A great king will need a strong army.

I love star wars and fighting. I'm a shooting star.

Lucy/Luke Star-Stamper is my name.

(He/she then inspects the row of stars)

What a horrible crowd of comets.

I'm going to get you fit.

You have to be fit to fight.

A million star jumps!

One, two, one two, jump, hup, hup.

(He/she spies someone not jumping)

Stop! Stop!

He/she marches across the stage towards two little stars, apparently eating chocolate.

Eating stars: Munch, munch, gobble, gobble, yum, yum.

Luke/Lucy: You two dozy sparks, come here.

Eating stars: Do we have to?

Luke/Lucy: Yes, double quick, one two, one two, halt.

What are you eating? *(Angry drill sergeant)*

Star 1: Galaxy, your honour.

Star 2: Mars, your toughness.

Lucy/Luke: Put them down, you murky meteors.

You have to be fit if you are ever going to be a black hole.

A sweet little star: Excuse me. Please Sir, b-b-but didn't the angel say he was going to be a Prince of Peace? He wants Peace on Earth.

Luke/Lucy: Peace, preposterous! Peace, pah! I'm off to burn up an atmosphere or two.

A glamorous film star steps forward

Film star: If he's going to be a prince, he will want rich and beautiful things: diamonds, rubies, sapphires, satins, silks and . . . me *(big flourish)*. I'm Stella Super Nova. The most beautiful film star, the loveliest starlet that ever had her name in lights. If he's a prince he will want me to look rich and glamorous; I will shine and glitter above his golden palace.

A little star: Palace? I heard he was going to be born in a stable.

The sweet star: Yes, and he's going to bring good news to the poor.

Film star: Poor – stable – how awful, how terrible. I'm not wasting my beauty on a stable. I've got my public to think about.

Little star: If he's going to change the world – this prince – he will be ever so clever.

Enter French football star.

Football star: Zen he weel want moi – I'm ever so clever – I know everything – people worship moi, like asteroids following ze Dog Star! I am ze deep space *(points to head)*.

Everyone chants: Ooh, Aah, Footballa,

Softer than a milky bar *(pointing to heads)*.

Little star: If you are so clever then you must have read Einstein.

Football star: Non.

Little star: You must have read Shakespeare.

Football star: Non, but I have red underpants *(shorts or whatever)*. I'm the greatest, I'm the best.

Little star: The angel says those who make themselves great will be humbled.

Football star: 'Umbled? 'Umbled? I weel not be zis 'umbled. I'm too great. I am off to where I'll be appreciated.

Everyone chants: Ooh, Ahh, Footballa,

Now you've really gone too far.

A pop star pushes forward.

Pop star: Look man, if he's like a great king, He's gonna want lots of fans.

I can show him. You've gotta be cool. Millions of people follow me.

I'm a pop star – Peter Andrex is my name.

I'm the King of Rock.

Little star: I've got your latest record: Twinkle, Twinkle Superstar.

Everyone: Twinkle, Twinkle Superstar

Lots of money and a big flash car.
Up upon the stage so bright
In your trousers, oh so tight.
Twinkle, Twinkle Superstar.
You're so lovely, you'll go far.

Pop star: Yeah, keep on twinkling, man.

All my fans keep me in comfort and luxury – the best food, wine, clothes.

Little star: The prophet says the King will suffer and everyone will turn on him. He will suffer to save everyone from their sins.

Pop star: What, suffer?

Suffer for other people? It's look after No. 1 in this business.

Little star: But a real king would care about others.

Pop star: Not me, man – I'm popping off if I've got to suffer.

Little star: I would love to be the chosen star if I was big enough.

He sounds like a king a star could really shine for.

Enter Angel.

Angel: God has chosen you, little star. You will shine beautifully.

The Little Star stands at the front of the stage with open arms. Mary, Joseph and Baby Jesus come down the aisle and sit below the star. Shepherds, sheep, kings, etc. join them. Silence. The end.

2.3 PEACE (EASTER)

A four-act play which could be performed as a single act of worship at Easter, or as four separate acts on successive days leading up to Easter. As it stands, this is only partially scripted; parts are left to the teacher or leader of worship to improvise, parts of Act 2 are to be mimed by the children, Act 3 is mainly undeveloped sketches which require improvisation by the children and Act 4 is a dramatic reading of the well-known 'death of Aslan' scene from C S Lewis's *The Lion, the Witch and the Wardrobe*.

Act 1: Escape to peace

Aim   Children to discover that to be at peace with others, we need to be at peace within ourselves.

Leader: (*Questions children*) How do we cope with feelings of anger, fear, loneliness, sadness, anxiety?

Do we go for a walk – be with friends – have a bath – listen to music – read a book?

Feeling all those emotions is like building a wall around ourselves that stops others from breaking in to us.

Drama Group (6–10 children): Mime grumpy, sad faces and build a wall around themselves with boxes covered with brown paper. Have labels with wording ANGER, FEAR, HATE, JEALOUSY, ENVY, LONELINESS stuck on boxes.

Leader: This doesn't make us feel too good – or those around us. We need to change and let other emotions break out.

Drama Group: Change boxes around to reveal that they have other words stuck on the other side: I'M SORRY, THANKS, KINDNESS, PLEASE FORGIVE ME, CARE, GENEROSITY, LOVE, FRIENDLINESS.

Leader: These feelings make us feel much better and help others to reach us.

Drama Group: Break down the wall – happy smiling faces – and go off with one another.

Leader: Let's sing 'Breakout' (C & P 91). Reads Bible verse (John 14.27) and asks children to think quietly as some children read their thoughts/prayers about coping with anger, frustration, etc.

Going-out music: 'Bridge over troubled water' (Simon & Garfunkel).

Act 2: Shout for peace

Aim   Sometimes we must be prepared to forgive – and not hold grudges.

Children show a collection of broken items – skirt, jumpers, toys, books, tyre, doll, etc., AND a collection of materials that repair – sellotape, glue, needle and thread, screwdriver, stapler, binding tape, stuffing.

Leader: Just like all these broken things – our friendship/relationships can be broken too – by our own words or actions. They need repairing – mending – just like these items. (*Points out mending items*)

Don't think these will be useful in our case – do you? Wonder what we can use?

Drama to be mimed as Leader tells story in own words of Jacob and Esau.

Summary

- Jacob robs Esau of his birthright.
- Jacob flees when Esau finds out.
- Jacob is tricked by Uncle Laban into marrying Leah instead of Rachel.
- Marries Rachel as well (seven years later again).
- Becomes wealthy.
- Feels sad about what he has done to his brother.
- Goes home to face his brother (frightened).
- Esau running towards him – crying, shouting – flinging arms around him with joy and happiness.

Leader: Jacob had what he most needed (*holds up placard above happy brothers Jacob and Esau – FORGIVENESS*).

Song: 'Make me a channel of your peace' (C & P 147), or 'Let there be love shared among us' (SoF 329)

Prayer

Children's own prayers on 'friends making up'.

Place placard – FORGIVENESS – with items that can be repaired, as a display to be left in the hall.

Act 3: Going for peace

Summary Sometimes we really do need to stand up for the peace way. Stand up to the bully. Not put up with bad behaviour. Stand up for the best way – the peace way.

Drama Group: Perform simple sketches and 'freeze' the sketch.

- At home scene – other people want to watch different programmes on TV.

- A brother/sister/friend wants to borrow a jumper/bike/personal stereo. One child says 'No, you never look after my things!' Argument.

- Mum/Dad/teacher asks person to do a quick job. Child grumbles/moans 'Oh, it's never . . . that gets to do jobs!' Argument.

Leader: Can you see yourself in any of these situations? Can you think of a suitable ending – for each scene? (*Drama Group will have already sorted out an ending*)

Drama Group: Acts again – with peaceful endings.

- At home.

- Lending belongings/possessions.

- Doing a job.

Another Group: Enters carrying headlines from the newspapers that tell of conflicts throughout the world.

Leader: All these places need peaceful settlements. We might not be able to do anything about them, but we can pray for peace – and peacemakers – pray for organizations that try to bring about peace, and help those suffering due to wars (*etc.*).

Song: 'Peace, perfect peace' (C & P 53).

Act 4: Broken for peace (for Easter)

Leader: Jesus has been called a bridge – because he tried to bring people and God together again. He was a bridge-builder.

Through his death on the cross – in a way we don't understand – he made a way for us to be friends again with God.

Drama Group/Children: Enact the death of Aslan from C S Lewis's book *The Lion, the Witch and the Wardrobe (this could be a whole class taking part, leader narrating – children miming).*

Leader: In the book, Aslan came back to life again, but not to be with the children. With that came a new feeling in the children – they had the courage and the spirit to go on to do the tasks Aslan had set for them.

Jesus died on a cross and came back to life again – but not to stay on earth. Instead, he said he would be here in a new way – to help us do the jobs we have to do for one another.

Music: (*Quietly playing*) 'Broken for me, broken for you' (HON 72)

Pray/Reflect

On people who have lost their lives helping others – rescuing others – saving others – on the sea – on the land.

Children could put symbols for peace on an Easter Tree as music quietly plays; symbols: crosses – rainbows – doves – United Nations white peace-keeping tanks – poppies (for remembrance).

2.4 EASTER

The significance of Easter may prove a difficult concept to put over to children. The aim of this script is to provide an opportunity for children to become aware of the conflicting forces of good and evil involved in the Easter event, and the meaning for a Christian's daily life of Jesus' victory over all that is bad.

Age range: Key Stage I

Resources

- A number of happy faces painted on one side of a card circle and, on the reverse sides, sad faces. These are used as masks on lengths of dowel.

- Lengths of green crêpe paper fastened on dowelling to be waved as palm branches.

- A triangle or similar suitable instrument for sounding as a signal for the reversing of the masks, and a child to play this.

- Eight copies of the script, one for each narrator and one for the instrumentalist.

The children taking part stand at the front of the hall facing the assembly. Those holding the palm branches stand at the back. The children with the masks stand in front of them. The narrators simply stand in the most suitable position. The triangle is sounded at the places indicated in the script either by * for the happy face or a # for the sad face. The children with masks show the happy face to begin with and reverse this when the triangle is played. The palm branches are waved during the singing of the song.

Entry music: 'Watch and pray', *Music of Taizé 1* (SDRM), 1982 recording available from St Thomas More Centre, The Burroughs, Hendon NW4 4TY; or 'O Lord, hear my

prayer' (HON 379), using the last few minutes.

Narrators (*reading a line each*):

Easter is about winning and losing. Christians believe it was a battle between good and evil.

So two faces are worn at Eastertime – the *good and # bad, the *happy and the #sad.

On the Sunday which begins what is known as Holy Week Jesus rode into Jerusalem on a donkey.

Crowds of people lined the roadway and children ran along shouting * 'Hosanna' as a welcome and waved palm branches.

Song: 'Trotting, trotting' (C & P 128)

Narrators: They were calling Jesus a King. They were happy.

But behind the crowds were bad men who were jealous of Jesus and who were plotting to put an end to him.#

The next day, Monday, Jesus went into the Temple in Jerusalem to pray.*

He noticed that the poor people were being cheated when they changed their money into Temple money.#

He was very angry with those who were being dishonest and unfair and drove them out of the Temple.

Many times people came to Jesus to ask him hard and sometimes silly questions.

Some wanted to know the answers so that they could lead better lives.*

But often they wanted to trick him.# Jesus always answered their questions in a wise way.

On the Thursday evening Jesus celebrated the Passover Festival with his friends.*

During the meal he told them that soon one of his friends would betray him to the bad men.*

Later that night Jesus was captured and taken away to be questioned. It was a sad and dark time for his friends.

Pontius Pilate, the Roman Governor, could not find Jesus guilty,* but was so scared of the bad men that he told the crowd he would let a prisoner go free because it was a festival time.

He thought the crowd would choose Jesus.

But they didn't.# Jesus was led away to die on a cross.

One of the two thieves at Jesus' side asked for forgiveness for all the bad things he had done.

Jesus promised that he would be with him in heaven.* Later that day, the Friday, Jesus died.#

Saturday was a very hard and sad day for Jesus' friends. It was a time of waiting.

On the Sunday Jesus' friends went to the tomb and to their amazement the huge stone covering the entrance was rolled away.

A man in white told them: 'He is risen!'* They rushed back to tell the others.

Later on the friends met the risen Jesus many times.

Song: 'Now the green blade rises' (C & P 131)

Narrators: Easter Sunday is a very joyful and important time of the year for Christians. They believe that Jesus came alive again and defeated death.

They are happy because he is still alive today and is their friend.

Prayer

> Our Father, at Easter time we remember all the things that happened to Jesus and his friends. How in the end Jesus died on a cross. There are times when we are sad and lonely, as they must have been. Help us to remember the promise of Easter and how happy the friends were when Jesus showed them that He was alive and would be with them for evermore. Amen.

Going-out music: 'Surrexit Christus' (MT 2).

3 Celebrating Christmas – again

Arguably the most popular, and the most hackneyed, topic for collective worship in primary schools is Christmas. Sometimes it seems that preparations for Christmas begin as soon as the embers of the Guy Fawkes bonfire die down. That we should celebrate the birth of our Lord, particularly in church schools, should need no justification, particularly when there is a danger of the festival being taken over by commercial interests and becoming a celebration of materialism and greed rather than one of incarnation and selflessness. One way of underlining the true purpose of Christmas is to switch the focus away from the traditional Nativity scene,

with its somewhat idealized stable, free of filth and squalor, its shepherds and kings and little donkeys on dusty roads, and look instead at ways in which people have celebrated Christmas at different times and in different places around the world.

Another very helpful approach is to tease apart the two separate accounts in Matthew and Luke. Matthew gives us the long genealogy, tracing the descent (genesis) of Jesus back through Joseph to Abraham; he refers to Jesus as 'Son of David, Son of Abraham' as an indication of his Jewish background. The angel then appears to Joseph, not Mary; no account is given of

the actual birth but, at some indeterminate point after the birth, the gentile 'Wise Men' (Magi) appear.

By contrast, Luke has the angel appearing to Mary, her kinsman Zechariah and the shepherds. Contrary to popular opinion, there is no mention of a stable, only that there was no room in the inn and the baby was laid in an ox's feeding trough.

We need to be very careful not to mix up these two accounts indiscriminately. Matthew has a particular reason for including his story of the Wise Men – he wants to emphasize the idea of powerful gentile leaders coming to worship Jesus, to underline his theme that Jesus was the fulfilment of God's promise to Abraham that all nations would be blessed through him. By contrast, Luke's humble scene with the baby in a cattle trough being visited by shepherds sets his theme of Jesus bearing the burdens of the lowly. If we conflate the two stories, written at different times and for different audiences, the themes may clash rather than complement each other.

Instead, why not use Luke's version in the run-up to Christmas, and Matthew's account of the visit of the Magi at the beginning of the Spring Term, as in 3.3?

Inevitably, the 'magic of Christmas' in its traditional form – the holly, the Christmas tree, the presents – is going to recur time after time, and this is not an attempt to abandon the joy of the traditional Christmas. Rather, it is an attempt to recapture something of the true 'magic' of Christmas and put it in ways that children can understand and celebrate: the amazing thought that somehow, in that birth at Bethlehem, 'God became man and dwelt among us'.

3.1 CHRISTMAS IS COMING

A traditional Christmas service with a difference – it contains elements of how Christmas was celebrated in times past, gives Christmas greetings in different languages to emphasize the world-wide spread of Christianity, and looks at Christmas customs and how they came about. The examples here of children's work on these topics are just that – examples! They are not necessarily to be used as they stand; much better if your children do their own research into Christmas customs and present their findings in their own words.

Candle is lit while the children walk in quietly to Christmas music.

Carol: 'Mary had a baby' (C & P 123)

Story of Christmas past

Children research beforehand by using reference books on Christmas long ago, and present a small sketch.

Christmas greetings

Younger children with cards give a variety of Christmas greetings in different languages e.g. Joyeux Noel – France; Houska Joulua – Finland.

Bell ringers play 'O come, O come Emmanuel'.

Narrator: Mary, a young girl who lived in Nazareth, near Lake Galilee, was engaged to Joseph, a skilled carpenter of the town, who could trace his ancestry back to King David.

One day when Mary was sitting at home, she had a very strange experience. It was like a dream; an angel, a messenger from God, appeared and spoke to her.

Messenger: Greetings, Mary. The Lord is with you.

Narrator: Mary was very puzzled by this. What could it all mean?

Messenger: Don't worry! The Lord God has chosen you for a special task. You are to have a son and you must call him Jesus. He is going to be a great man; the people will call him Son of the Most High God. He will be given the throne of David, and will be king of Israel for ever.

Narrator: The vision faded away, and Mary was left rubbing her eyes and wondering if it had really happened.

Song: 'The Virgin Mary' (C & P 121)

Reader 1: Some time later, when Joseph and Mary were married and it was nearly time for Mary's baby to be born, the Roman Emperor Augustus ordered that everyone in the empire should go to their home town to be registered in a census. Joseph came from the village of Bethlehem, near Jerusalem, so even though Mary was pregnant, they had to make the long journey there.

Reader 2: They arrived late at night, and Joseph set about finding somewhere to stay. Of course, many other people were travelling at the time because of the Roman census, and all the rooms were taken. Joseph and Mary had to spend the night in an outhouse at the back of the inn, sharing it with the cattle and donkeys. Later that night, in the squalor and filth of the stable, Mary's baby was born.

Reader 3: Knowing that the baby was due soon, Mary had brought with her swaddling clothes – bands of cloth that people used at the time – to wrap the baby in. When he was securely wrapped up, she laid him gently in a bed of straw in a manger, and she and Joseph settled down to try and get some rest.

Reader 4: Not far away, on the hillside near the village, shepherds were looking after their flocks. They were sitting round a fire, chatting or dozing, when suddenly they were dazzled by a great light in the sky. They were terrified, but a reassuring voice spoke to them and calmed their fears.

Voice: Don't be afraid! I bring you good news. A baby has been born in Bethlehem who will be the Messiah, the new David you have all been waiting for. Go into Bethlehem at once, and you will find the baby wrapped in swaddling clothes, lying in a manger.

Reader 5: It seemed to the astonished shepherds that they could hear singing: a great chorus of sound, like an angelic choir, singing praises to God. Then the light faded from the sky, and the sound was no more.

Reader 6: Scrambling to their feet, the shepherds left their flocks and ran excitedly into the village. They soon found the stable and gazed in awe and wonder at the tiny baby, fast asleep in the manger. Some of them fell on their knees and worshipped him. They told their story to everyone who would listen. People were amazed and thought they were out of their minds, but Mary remembered the words of the messenger from God, smiled to herself, and hugged the baby tightly to her breast.

Carol: 'Away in a Manger' (JP 12)

The following ideas are suggestions, to be developed if thought appropriate, and if time permits:

● Christmas food – display younger children's drawings of Christmas food and say what they are.

● Story of Christmas present: children research beforehand 'Christmas today' (using reference books) and present a small sketch.

● Christmas cards and presents: children's own designs and presents of long ago and now.

● Story of Christingle.

● Story of Prince Albert and the first Christmas tree; children research story beforehand.

3.2 CHRISTMAS – THE GREATEST GIFT

A simple act of worship, starting with obvious and readily available visual aids – a decorated Christmas tree and a nicely wrapped present – and going on to underline the real message of Christmas.

Leader: I wonder how many children have their Christmas trees up at home. Last night ours went up and already members of the family are starting to put exciting parcels underneath. In fact, I have borrowed one of these to bring in to show you this morning. Can someone come and read what the gift tag says? 'To Matthew, with love from Nana.' Yes, and Matthew has already spied it and he's trying to guess what it might be. Can you guess? (*Children offer guesses*)

I remember when our children were much smaller and Christmas morning was a very noisy and hectic time. The children would rush downstairs and dive straight into all the parcels, ripping off the coloured rosettes and ribbons, tearing at the paper, and then – almost without worrying about what was inside – they were on to the next one and the next one and the next. Sometimes, it was only later, when all the paper had gone and everything had quietened down, that the children really looked at the presents that had been in the parcels.

I'm sure Christmas can be a bit like that for all of us sometimes. We look forward to putting up our tree. We get excited about the Christmas party. We wonder if our parents will enjoy our Christmas concert.

Then, when Christmas Eve finally comes, we wonder

– If we will get the presents we want

– If the Christmas dinner will be tasty

– If the films on the telly will be good.

But really, all those things are like the wrapping paper, the rosettes and the ribbons around the present. We can so easily forget about the greatest gift of Christmas.

Because the real reason that we celebrate Christmas is God giving the most wonderful gift to the world. That gift is Jesus, and it is God's way of showing just how much he loves us, because Jesus is God's very precious and only Son.

Bible text: John 3.16

Songs: 'At this time of giving' (SoF 33); 'This Child' (JP 480)

Prayer

> Generous God, we thank you for all the exciting things we can enjoy at Christmas, and for those who work so hard to make it such a special time for us. Thank you most of all for the gift of your Son, Jesus, the greatest gift we could ever know. Amen.

3.3 EPIPHANY BLESSING OF THE SCHOOL

A simple service based on a South German custom. This rounds off the Christmas season. If it takes place at the beginning of the Spring Term, it 'distances' the story of the Magi from the birth narrative and puts it in its proper context.

Leader: It is a South German tradition to bless homes at Epiphany. In this act of worship we bless the school for the coming year.

The leader explains that in South Germany, there would be a great procession around the village. Here in school, in Britain, we just process the three kings/queens around the hall during the singing of a suitable Epiphany carol. The whole school has gathered together. The three kings/queens (three reception children dressed in appropriate robes and carrying wrapped gifts) walk into the hall and stand at the front.

The leader rehearses the biblical story of the Magi (Matthew chapter 2) in his/her own words, omitting or playing down the massacre of the innocents, and explains that wise people will search out the will of God and try to do it in their lives. To follow God's way – like the kings/queens followed the star – brings us into the presence of Jesus. To walk God's way brings great blessings – just as the Magi were blessed by being led into the presence of the holy family.

Prayer

> We pray that all members of our school community will try and seek out God's will and walk his way during the coming year.

Leader: In Germany a blessing is chalked above the door of each house during the great procession around the village. Instead, we have prepared a painted blessing which is going to be placed in the window above the main entrance to the school. In 1999, this is:

19 + C + M + B + 99

The numerals represent the new year; the four 'plus' signs represent the four seasons of the coming year; the letters are for the names of the three magi: C = Caspar, M = Melchior and B = Balthasar.

Song: 'We three kings' (JP 271)

During this song, the three kings/queens process round the hall, carrying their gifts.

Prayer of blessing for the school

God of all time and space, may this school be filled with kindness to one another, with hospitality to guests, and with abundant care for every visitor during the coming year. By the gentle light of a star, guide home all who seek you on paths of wonder, peace and love, where we will join with the angels in proclaiming your praise: Glory to God in the highest and peace on earth now and for ever. Amen.

An Advent/Christmas/Epiphany calendar which ends on 6 January may be used – available from Kevin Mayhew Publications. Children come up each day and open the doors and describe the image which is revealed, e.g. three kings on 6 January.

Another epiphany prayer may be used:

Let us pray. God of epiphanies, we give you thanks for Jesus, who reveals your glory. Open our eyes to the surprises that are your gifts to us each day. In Jesus' name we pray. Amen.

The act of worship may end with the following words:

Leader: Epiphany is a day of great rejoicing! For those who have kept the days of Advent and the twelve days of Christmastime, Epiphany is a day of fulfilment.

Epiphany is a triple celebration of Jesus' showing forth: the adoration of the Magi, the baptism of Jesus, and water becoming wine at the wedding feast in Cana.

Epiphany is a day for festive celebration. Make your homes glitter with gold and make them smell fragrantly of frankincense and myrrh. Use your creativity to make this day a high point in your household. Make stars to brighten your windows. In honour of the Magi, make crowns that can be worn by kings and queens. Give the last Christmastime gifts on this day when gifts were offered to the Christ Child.

3.4 THE SHEPHERDS' SEARCH

Age range: Key Stage 1

Introductory music: Any form of Christmas music should be playing as the school comes in. A carol with a shepherd theme would be most appropriate.

Explain that one of the things done at Christmas is that people look for things. It might be that while we are sitting here, someone is out looking for a present for us. When we think we won't get caught, we might go looking to see if we can find out what we have been bought. Children can be asked to share where they look in their house for their presents. It can be stated that even on that very first Christmas lots of people were looking. They weren't looking for their presents but for a baby who they had been told was the best present the world would ever get.

Story: The shepherds' search

It was the angels' fault. 'Go and find a king,' they said. 'You will find him lying in a manger in a stable in Bethlehem,' they had said. But Bethlehem was full of stables – and full of mangers.

The shepherds decided to split up to search. 'We'll meet at the inn,' they said.

The first shepherd tried all the mangers in the first street. He found hay . . . and straw . . . and some eggs . . . but no baby.

The second shepherd tried all the mangers in the second street. He found a dog . . . a cat . . . and some chickens . . . but no baby.

The third shepherd tried all the mangers in the third street. He found some hungry animals . . . some friendly animals . . . and some very friendly animals . . . but no baby.

They all met at the inn.

'No luck!' they all said together. They sat down. They were very miserable.

Suddenly, the first shepherd called out. 'What's that?' he said, pointing to a stable they hadn't seen before.

'What's that?' said the second shepherd, pointing to a large star over their heads.

'What's that?' said the third shepherd, hearing a baby's cry. The shepherds looked at each other and ran into the stable.

There was a baby lying in the manger. The shepherds knelt down, their faces beaming. 'We've been looking everywhere!' said the shepherds. 'And now we've found him!'

(This simple story lends itself to illustrations, which could be drawn beforehand on large sheets of paper by older pupils, or on overhead projector transparencies, and displayed at the appropriate point.)

Explain that with everything that goes on at Christmas, sometimes Jesus can get lost again, and you have to look really hard for him. The shepherds searched because the angels said Jesus was very important and would bring light to a dark world. It's really important for Christians that Jesus is found at Christmas because of all the darkness there is left in the world. Christians believe that it is a time to celebrate the light that came into the world that day and mustn't get lost.

Prayer

A time of silent reflection could be held as children think about where they would like light to shine, either in their own lives or in the world. These issues could be raised by the leader, or the class if it was being led by children.

Hymn: Any appropriate Christmas carol, e.g. 'While shepherds watched their flocks by night' (JP 285)

4 Making Bible stories come alive

Many acts of collective worship contain a reading from the Bible or a reference to the Bible. They don't have to, of course; there are plenty of examples in this book which do not! But the Bible is such an important part of worship in the Christian Church that it seems sensible to make use of it regularly in collective worship in school as well.

Another good reason for including the Bible in collective worship is that with the growth of the multi-faith approach to RE, far less

Bible is taught in RE nowadays than used to be the case. Not that this is necessarily a bad thing; RE is now much broader, and anyway in the days of the old Bible-based RE syllabuses, we used to try and do far too much, too soon (the 1964 Lindsey Agreed Syllabus had 228 Bible passages to be taught in Key Stage 1!). We need to be sure that we don't repeat that mistake when selecting Bible stories for collective worship in primary schools. Remember, the Bible is a library of books covering a period of some 1,200 years or more; it was written for adult believers; and it is very controversial – wars have been fought over its meaning and churches have split over the nature of its authority.

So:

- Be selective. Think about the effect the story will have on children. Do you really want children to think that God sends floods to wipe out humanity? If you tell the story of Noah to five-year-olds, that's what you're doing.

- Do use a modern translation, or tell the story in your own words. What would a child make of 'And the child grew, and waxed strong in spirit'?

- Do be sure that you understand the theological significance of the story. For example, is the Feeding of the 5,000 really a miracle story? Remember, Jesus rejected the temptation to turn stones into bread.

- Do be aware of the historical setting. How many versions of the Good Samaritan totally miss the point? The Samaritans were the enemies of the Jews, and Jesus was saying 'Love your enemies.'

- Do make the story come alive.

Other chapters deal with scripted drama, improvised drama, re-enacting the life of Jesus; here are some examples of other ways of presenting the Bible in worship.

4.1 BUBBLES (UNKIND WORDS)

An example of an act of worship which makes a powerful contribution to the children's spiritual, moral and social development, and uses Bible passages as examples of the wounding effects of insults and taunts.

Age range: Key Stage 1

Resources Children's bubble mixture (washing-up liquid is not as good).

Context Particularly useful when there have been incidents of bad language and unkind words to others in the school.

Introductory music: *La Mer* by Debussy.

The leader greets the children.

Song: 'I'm forever blowing bubbles'

Bible reading

A reading about the soldiers and the crowd jeering at the helpless Jesus at his crucifixion, from Luke 22.63-65 and Luke 23.35-40:

The soldiers first took Jesus down to the courtyard, and began to mock him. They dressed him in a purple robe like a king, forced a rough crown of thorns on his head, and pretended to salute him.

'Hail, king of the Jews!' they jeered, beating him and spitting on him. Then they put the cross-bar over his shoulders, and led him away to the place of execution.

The crowd mocked and jeered at Jesus as he hung helpless on the cross, his body racked with pain.

'He saved others, but can't save himself!' they cried. 'If you really are the Messiah, come down from the cross – then we'll believe you!'

(These short passages lend themselves to dramatic reading. A group of older pupils could read the insulting and taunting verses chorally.)

The leader talks to the children about school incidents in the class or the playground that have been noticed or brought to staff

notice. A chat to the staff beforehand may help you glean more information. Perhaps there are children in school who are bullied, teased, less able, or very quiet, who are the butts of insensitive children. Question the children. Even if you are sorry, can unkind words or deeds be retrieved? How do you feel when someone says something unpleasant to you? Get a good dialogue going. After a short period, stop.

Get the children to sit on their hands (hands in laps tend to wander upwards automatically!). Ask for absolute silence until you have finished what you are about to do. Produce the bubble mixture and, using the wand, walk around the children blowing copious bubbles. The children must not catch the bubbles or move. Go to the front, taking a child with you. Blow more bubbles down the room or hall and then ask the chosen child to go and catch one and bring it to you. Of course the bubble bursts (hopefully!) before the child can return one to you. Do this two or three times. Appear incredulous that they are unable to do it. Tell the children that words are like bubbles that cannot be retrieved once you have let them go. Therefore what they say should not be said thoughtlessly, hurtfully or unkindly. Bad words should never be set free. Being sorry is insufficient because often words live on inside people and affect them for a long time – sometimes for life.

Hymn: 'Magic penny' (A 10)

Prayer

> Dear Father, help me to think about the words I use when I speak to people. May I never say cruel or hurtful things. Help me notice when people are unhappy and sad so that I may use words to cheer them up. May I do this for your sake. Amen.

Concluding music: *La Mer* by Debussy.

Follow-up in class

Ask the children to draw large bubbles and put relevant words in them. Make a collage to remind them of the assembly.

Final note: Do not blow any bubbles apart from those needed. If you blow some afterwards you will lose the impact of the assembly.

4.2 WATER INTO WINE

A difficult story, this, because it is only found in the Fourth Gospel, not in the Synoptics, and scholars disagree about its historical veracity. Probably better for Key Stage 2, where the question of the point of the story can be discussed afterwards in class. The dramatic effect of the food colouring will be quite a talking point – but beware of the danger of turning Jesus into a magician! The follow-up discussion is really important here.

The story lends itself well to dramatization, with four readers.

Age range: Key Stage 2

Resources (if required) One glass jug of water, one wine glass with a small amount of food colouring in the bottom.

Context Link to a family theme, e.g. baptisms, weddings, etc., or even after a member of staff has got married!

Introductory music: 'Wedding March' from *A Midsummer Night's Dream* by Mendelssohn.

The leader greets the children and talks to them about their experience of weddings. Why are they happy occasions? What happens at a wedding? Are there things that could possibly go wrong (e.g. forget rings, etc.)?

Bible reading

The wedding at Cana (John 2.1-11). This story may be told in your own words or in the following version:

John wondered how he could possibly explain to his friends just how big a change Jesus had made in his life. He told them a story to try to make it clear to them.

'Once upon a time, Jesus went to a wedding with his disciples. Everything went smoothly until, halfway through the wedding feast, the wine ran out. Jesus' mother, who had also been invited, came up to Jesus and asked him if he could do anything about it. He didn't want to help at first, I could tell. He said something about not being ready. But his mother wouldn't take no for an answer, and Jesus ordered the servants to fill up six stone water-jars with water. They couldn't see any point in that, and Mary had to speak quite sharply to them to make them do what Jesus asked. Anyway, they went off grumbling and filled the jars, and then Jesus told them to draw some off and take it to the master of ceremonies. He tasted it, and declared it was better than the wine they had served up at first. This is the first clue that I'm going to give you about Jesus.'

(Use great expression, if told by one voice. Alternatively, dramatize the reading, with one reader for Jesus, one for Mary, one for the steward, and one for the narrator.)

Try to let the children see how mystified the servants were when Jesus told them to fill jars with water. When you come to the point where the servant pours water into a glass, pour water from a jug into the wine glass. The red colouring will make it look like wine. Allow time for silence, awe and wonder, scepticism. Talk about Jesus having saved the day.

Hymn: 'Jesus' hands were kind hands' (SSL 33)

Prayer

Dear Jesus, thank you that you are interested in every part of our lives. You cared about the bridegroom in the story and helped him with his problem. We know that when we have difficulties you help us too. Let us spend a few minutes in silence and if any of you have a problem that you would like Jesus to help you with, then think of it now in your mind, quietly. (*Pause for 30 seconds*) Please help us all with any difficulties we have. Amen.

Concluding music: 'Wedding March' from *A Midsummer Night's Dream* by Mendelssohn.

Follow-up in the classroom

What do the children think is the point of the story? Explain how John, the author of the Fourth Gospel, used a number of signs to mark key points in the narrative. Here he was explaining, in story form, that the rich red 'wine' of Christianity was replacing the thin, ineffective 'water' of Jewish rituals. (Note verse 6 – the six stone water jars were 'of the kind used for Jewish rites of purification'. This is a pretty strong clue!) This doesn't mean it didn't happen; it means the importance of the story, to John, lies in what it signifies, not whether it actually took place.

4.3 COMMUNICATION

In this act of worship, the theme of communication is central, and the first Bible extract – the story of the tower of Babel – is used incidentally, as a kind of humorous interlude. The second Bible passage, Jesus' teaching on prayer, serves a quite different purpose. It introduces the idea of prayer as a different kind of communication – communication with God. This could be usefully followed up in class, or in a subsequent act of worship. (See also Chapter 7, 'Different approaches to prayer'.)

Opening: Children sing 'Kum ba yah' as it is an easy hymn to sing using sign language (C & P 68).

Leader: What is communication?

A group of children spell out the word 'communication' using large decorated

letters and show pictures of all the different ways by which we can communicate with each other, e.g. computer, telephone, sign language, braille.

Story: The Tower of Babel (Genesis 11.1-9):

Once upon a time when the world was young, all mankind spoke the same language – a simple language with very few words, which would sound to us more like grunts. Many people were nomads; that is, they wandered from place to place with their sheep and goats, looking for water and grazing land. One group of people arrived at a fertile plain between two great rivers, which we call the Tigris and the Euphrates. Here they pitched camp for a while.

One night, they were sitting round the camp fire talking among themselves.

'Soon be time we were moving on,' said one.

'Why should we?' said another. 'The grass is still good, why don't we just stay here?'

'Good idea,' said his wife. 'I'm tired of packing everything up and walking for miles. There's plenty of clay and mud here on the river banks. Why don't we build proper houses, like we saw in the town?'

And so it was decided. They built houses of baked mud, and soon had a flourishing township. But the building didn't stop there.

'You know, this building with mud bricks is really quite easy,' one of the men said to his friends one night. 'Why don't we build ourselves a temple with a tower? We could keep on building it up and up, right to the sky. We could reach the heavens!'

'That's right!' the others cried excitedly. 'We could get to where God lives! We could be like him!'

It was the same old story, Adam and Eve all over again, men wanting to be like gods. They rushed backwards and forwards, chattering excitedly, carrying piles of hard-baked mud bricks, and soon the tower was so high that the top was nearly out of sight in the clouds. From his home in the heavens, Yahweh looked on in dismay.

'What are they up to now?' he asked himself. 'I kept them out of the garden after Adam and Eve let me down – now they're climbing up to my backyard! What am I to do with them?'

Frowning, Yahweh went down to the town and walked unseen among the busy builders, watching them working and listening as they shouted orders to one another. Suddenly, he had an idea.

'That's it!' he said to himself. 'I'll muddle up their speech, and make them all speak different languages. They won't be able to understand each other, and they'll never be able to work together on this silly tower. Then perhaps I'll get some peace.'

No sooner had Yahweh thought it, than it was done. The men and women at work on the tower suddenly began to speak in different languages. No one could understand what had happened. Each person thought he was speaking the same language as everyone else and couldn't think why the others were talking gibberish. They shouted angrily at one another, fists began to fly, mud bricks tumbled down from the top of the scaffolding, and before long they all gave up and went angrily home. The happy township split up, and the families went off in different directions, each speaking their own language.

And that, the story says, is why the city on that site is known as Babylon – because there God made the speech of men into a babble of different languages.

(This story is an attempt to explain why men of different races or tribes speak different languages. The storyteller probably has in mind the ziggurats, great temple-towers, the remains of which may still be found in the Tigris–Euphrates valley. The story could easily be dramatized as it is read, with children using cardboard boxes to build the tower.)

Sign language

The teacher and children teach the audience some simple signs for cow, sheep, pig and horse so that the whole school can join in with the following song.

Song: 'Old MacDonald had a farm' – sung and signed by children

Time may then be spent focusing on written communication. Children hold up large examples of:

- a letter
- a diary
- a postcard
- a shopping list
- an invitation.

The leader gives the audience clues about the type of written message, e.g. you could write it to friends back home if you were at the seaside.

Children then read out some of their own descriptive writing – 'Messages in a Bottle'.

Leader: The earliest form of communication was communicating with pictures. Here are some early examples of cave paintings. What do you think they mean? (*Allow discussion at this point*)

Children show their own cave paintings (done with chalk, charcoal, soil, crushed berries, twigs, onion skin, etc.). They explain how they made their own painting.

Bible reading

Matthew 6.5-15, Jesus' teaching on prayer. This is quite difficult, and is perhaps best read by a teacher.

Prayer

Finally, children read their own thank you prayers to God, e.g.:

My Thank You Prayer!
Dear Lord, I thank you for all the good
 things in life.
Thank you for the fresh waters. The
 animals you gave us.
I thank you for our friends who play
 with us and the beautiful
 pictures and our talents. Amen.

4.4 LIGHT

A simple, moving act of worship which graphically illustrates another of John's great 'signs' – this time, the sign of Jesus, the Light of the World. Later, this is linked to a verse from the Psalms; this could be followed up in class, to reinforce the idea of continuity between Old Testament and New Testament.

Resources A collection of sources of light, e.g. torch, candle, lantern, miner's lamp. Part of the time the room might be darkened.

Leader: Jesus said, 'I am the light of the world. The person who follows me will never live in darkness. He will have the light which gives life' (John 8.12). What did he mean by this? (*Children give answers*)

Ask what light does. Ask children for some suggestions, e.g.:

- Helps us to see in the dark, because dark cannot kill light (lights; torches).

- Helps to show us the way (cat's eyes; torches).

- Helps to keep us out of danger (light-houses).

- Helps things to grow (sun).

- Sun shining through windows shows up dirt and dust.

Leader: So Jesus means that he helps us to do all these things – to see things which need to be done to help others; to show us the way to live; to help to keep us out of danger; to help us to grow closer to God; and help us to see the things which we do that are wrong.

He gives his light to his followers and we can be light to others.

The Bible says 'Your word is like a lamp for my feet and a light for my ways' (Psalm 119. 105). (*Expand if time*)

Prayer

Light the 'thinking candle' for prayer/reflection; prayers written by the children could be included here, or these prayers from the Iona Community:

Reader 1: I will light a light

In the name of the Maker

Who lit the world

And breathed the breath of life for me.

(*A candle is lit and placed centrally*)

Reader 2: I will light a light

In the name of the Son

Who saved the world

And stretched out his hand for me.

(*A candle is lit and placed centrally*)

Reader 3: I will light a light

In the name of the Spirit

Who encircles the world

And blesses my soul with longing.

(*A candle is lit and placed centrally*)

Reader 4: We will light three lights

For the Trinity of love

God above us

God beside us

God beneath us

The beginning

The end

The everlasting one.

(John L. Bell from *A Wee Worship Book*, Wild Goose Worship Group, 1989)

(*A moment of silence is kept*)

Song: 'This little light of mine' (JP 258)

4.5 MOVING MOUNTAINS

A powerful Old Testament story, Gideon driving out the Midianites (Judges chapter 7) is retold dramatically in the teacher's own words, with illustrative mime by a group of children, and given a contemporary interpretation: with faith, anything is possible.

Entrance music: 'God's great banana skin' by Chris Rea.

The leader welcomes school.

Song: 'He's got the whole world' (C & P 19)

Leader: Introduces theme with thoughts on:

- What we can all do – attend school, walk, sit, think, etc.

- What we can do tomorrow.

- What we can't do yet.

- What we find personally difficult or can't do at all.

Some children speak in turn, and share their own personal thoughts:

- Things I know will happen tomorrow – sunrise, sunset, no school (Saturday).

- Things I'll do in the future – ride my bike, take part in a swimming gala, etc.

- Things I can't do very well – read, write with pen, tell the time, run, tests at school. Coping with illness in the family. Death of a pet/family member.

Leader: In the Bible, a man was faced with an enormous problem. He had to overcome a great enemy, the Midianities, who had captured his city. God had told him to get rid of them. Gideon was only a little man and he felt quite weak.

Children now mime the story with minimal props. A small helpless boy, representing Gideon, stands up and looks bemused.

Leader: Tells story in own words. God told Gideon to disperse the army he had managed to round up – army depleting. The men who wanted to return home – go. The men who . . . etc. Until poor Gideon had a few brave men left, after starting with thousands. God told Gideon of his plan.

Gideon mimes listening. A group of children stand with Gideon, using paper horns as trumpets, any percussion instruments that are available and ready to shout the slogan 'for God and for Gideon'.

Leader: These men surrounded the city at dead of night and banged their instruments (*mime*) and blew their trumpets (*mime*) and shouted their loudest (*mime*) and the Midianites were terrified – so terrified that they fled the other way from what they thought was a vast army.

Gideon had won a battle he had thought was impossible to win. With God, everything – anything – is possible. He can move mountains.

Prayer

Dear God, thank you for people whom we can trust, especially mums, dads, teachers and our friends. Thank you that we can always trust you. Amen.

Thank you, God, for all the people we live with and everyone who cares for us. Amen.

Children listen to the opening piece of music as they lead out.

5 Re-enacting the life of Jesus

The first thing to emphasize here is that we never can re-enact the life of Jesus. The Gospels are not, and were not intended to be, biographies. They were written many years after Jesus' death, and although their authors may well have had access to eye-witnesses to the events they describe, they themselves were probably not eyewitnesses.

Secondly, the evangelists were writing for specific audiences; Luke, for example, was writing for the Gentiles (non-Jews), and his Gospel does rather tend to put the Jews in a bad light. Matthew, by contrast, writing for Jews, deploys the so-called 'argument from prophecy' quite extensively, quoting from the Old Testament to 'prove' that Jesus really was the Messiah the Jews had been expecting.

Thirdly, remember the setting: first-century Palestine, harsh Roman occupation, high expectations of a Messiah who would throw out the Romans and set up a new Israel with the Jewish people vindicated, plenty of false Messiahs around, a general belief in demon-possession and many people going about who could cure by 'casting out demons'. It is in this setting, so alien to twentieth-century Britain, that we have to try and re-enact the life of Jesus to mean something to our children. It is not an easy task. It should, however, inspire us to do our homework – to read the New Testament and the commentaries, to study more history and theology, to realize the inadequacy of just 'telling the stories', and to improve the quality of what we teach the children, both in RE and in collective worship.

These acts of worship are a contribution to that process. (See also Chapters 2, 'Celebrating Christmas'; 4, 'Making Bible stories come alive'; 10, 'Writing and telling stories'; and 12, 'Red Letter Days'.)

5.1 PALM SUNDAY

This is one in a series of acts of worship leading up to Easter. There is scope for simple drama (different kinds of greetings for different occasions), use of artwork (flags from different countries) and language (greetings from different countries), and further dramatic presentations (ways of greeting an important visitor). Finally, there is opportunity for the leader of the worship to exercise his/her story-telling skills by retelling Luke's account of the entry into Jerusalem in his/her own words.

Note In preparing to tell this story, do look carefully at what Luke says! It was Jesus' disciples, according to Luke, not the crowd, who interpreted Jesus' actions as those of a king, coming in peace, and who praised God 'for all the great things they had seen'.

Introduction

Explain that since it is the beginning of the week, you would like to greet everyone properly this morning and make sure everyone is OK. Start by greeting one another, move on to greeting other staff, then parents, then year groups in the school and finally a 'Good morning, everyone'.

Explain that the way you greet someone says a lot about what you think of them. Various scenes could then be played by children: how do best friends greet each other, how do enemies greet each other, how do long lost relatives greet each other, etc.

It can then be explained that all over the world, people have different ways of greeting each other. A number of different greetings from around the world can then be shared, with children perhaps showing a flag of a particular country and then that country's greeting can be said and repeated by the school. Some dialects such as 'Ay up, me duck' could also be included.

It can then be said that if you were having to greet someone very important, there might be lots of things you would have to do. (*Children can be used as models to show each of these things*)

First, you would have to look smart. Put on some posh clothes, brush your teeth and comb your hair.

Secondly, you would have to learn to bow properly, so that when the important person came by, you would know what to do.

Lastly, you would have to practise what you were going to say so that you wouldn't be

tongue-tied when you actually met them. Then you would be ready. This sequence could end with the children who had been demonstrating these actions coming before the leader of worship in turn, and doing and saying what they would do for the hypothetical important visitor.

Bible reading

The story of Palm Sunday (Luke 19.28–38) is now told by the leader of worship, in his/her own words, or as follows:

The story of Palm Sunday is all about Jesus being greeted by lots of people. Jesus and the disciples reached the village of Bethany on the Mount of Olives, close to Jerusalem. It was just before the great Festival of Passover, and the roads near Jerusalem were thronged with pilgrims going up to the city to celebrate the festival.

Jesus stopped at a house in Bethany where he had friends, and sent two of his disciples on to the next village.

'When you get to the village,' he told them, 'you'll find a donkey tethered to the fence. It's a young donkey, which has never been ridden. Unhitch it, and bring it back here. If anyone asks you what you're doing, just say, "The master needs it – we'll bring it back tomorrow." It'll be all right – it's all arranged.'

The disciples went straight away, and found the young donkey tied up outside a house in the main street of the village, just as Jesus had said. They untied it and started leading it off down the street.

'Hey! Where do you think you're going?' a voice cried out suddenly. It was the owner of the house, standing in the doorway.

'The master needs it,' they replied, as Jesus had told them.

'The master, eh?' the man replied. 'I guess that's all right, then. Mind you bring the donkey back, though.'

They went back to Bethany with the donkey, and Jesus came out to meet them.

'Ah, good, you've found it,' he said. 'I'm going to ride into Jerusalem so that everyone knows who I am. Come on, get ready.'

The disciples spread their cloaks on the donkey's back, and Jesus sat on the makeshift saddle. With the disciples leading the way, Jesus rode into Jerusalem. The road was crowded with pilgrims, and all along the way people were throwing down brushwood cut from the fields, and branches of palm trees. They were greeting all the pilgrims with verses from the Psalms: 'Blessed are those who come in the name of the Lord: blessings on the kingdom of David.'

No one took any notice of Jesus in particular; as far as the people of Jerusalem were concerned, he was just another pilgrim who had come up for the festival. Little did they know that they were greeting the man who in himself brought the new kingdom of David.

Disappointed, Jesus dismounted from the donkey, and handed the reins to one of his disciples.

'That's it, I'm afraid,' he said. 'Nobody wants to know us today. Take the donkey back, and I'll think of another way to show them who I am.'

The important thing to remember is that not everyone there that day understood what was going on, and not everyone was cheering. There was also a group of Pharisees, important religious people of the time, who believed that Jesus was wrong and they were getting more and more cross. They knew they were going to have to do something about him.

As the story goes on, you are going to hear more about the crowds and more about the Pharisees. You will see the crowds make a choice about who they are going to listen to, Jesus or the Pharisees. I wonder who you would listen to if you were there?

Summary

Explain that on Palm Sunday, the disciples welcomed Jesus as their king. Christians

today still believe Jesus is their King and they sing songs to welcome him just as they did in those days.

Song: 'Make way, make way' (SoF 384)

5.2 THE CRUCIFIXION

This follows on from the Palm Sunday worship. The story of the crucifixion is, of course, difficult to tell to young children, and this act of worship concentrates on the disciples' worries and fears, and relates these to the children's own personal 'worry monster'. The worship ends on a positive note, with the 'worry monsters' being screwed up and thrown away as a demonstration of good overcoming evil.

Introduction

Draw three faces: one happy, one straight and one sad. Ask the children which one they felt like when they got to school that morning. Have a show of hands. Next, ask them to give examples of what might make them feel like one of those faces.

When it gets to the sad face, ask the children to think about those things that make them sad. Say that sometimes what makes people unhappy is that they are worrying about what might happen in the future. Read 'Whatif' by Shel Silverstein (from *A Light in the*

Attic, HarperCollins, 1981). This could just be read straight, alternating between readers, or some of it could be done dramatically by children as it is read.

Next, show a picture of a monster (this could have been drawn by children). Explain that this is a worry monster. It rears its ugly head and makes you feel scared and unhappy. Children can then come up with things that make them worried or unhappy or scared and they can be stuck around the monster.

Bible reading

Explain that Good Friday was a day when Jesus' disciples were very worried and sad. First, they had let Jesus down.

The story of Peter's betrayal could be read (Luke 22.54-61) or retold in the teacher's own words (see version given in 6.1).

Secondly, they had seen the crowds turn on Jesus, just a few days after they had cheered him.

The story of Jesus in front of Pilate could then be read (Luke 23.1-5) or retold as follows:

Next morning, the chief priests took Jesus in chains before Pilate, the Roman governor.

'This man claims to be king of the Jews,' they said. 'We demand the death penalty. If you won't execute him, you are no friend of Caesar.'

Pilate had Jesus brought before him.

'Is this true?' he asked.

'The words are theirs,' Jesus replied. And to Pilate's surprise, Jesus would not say any more.

Pilate knew that the chief priest and religious leaders were trying to force his hand, and he looked for a loophole in the law. Every year, at the Passover Festival, the Governor used to release one prisoner to the crowd. Pilate went out on the balcony, and spoke to the pilgrims in the square.

'Shall I release Jesus, the king of the Jews?' he asked them.

The chief priests had planted men among the crowd, and they began to shout for Barabbas to be set free instead. Barabbas was a Jewish nationalist who had been arrested by the Romans for rebellion.

The crowd took up the cry. 'Barabbas! We want Barabbas!' they yelled.

Pilate was taken aback. 'What shall I do with this man Jesus?' he asked.

'Crucify him!' a voice cried out. 'Yes, yes, crucify him! Crucify!' the crowd roared.

Pilate had not the courage to stand against a mob. Meekly he signed the death penalty, and Jesus was led away to be executed, while Barabbas was released.

Finally, they had seen their best friend put to death.

A summary of the crucifixion could be told:

They came to the hill called Golgotha, which means 'the place of the skull'. Then he was nailed to the cross, and the cross was hoisted upright. The soldiers divided his clothes among themselves by throwing dice. They wrote down the charge against him and put it on the cross: 'THE KING OF THE JEWS'. Two criminals were crucified at the same time, one either side of Jesus.

The crowd mocked and jeered at Jesus as he hung helpless on the cross, his body racked with pain.

'He saved others, but can't save himself!'

they cried. 'If you really are the Messiah, come down from the cross – then we'll believe you!'

At midday, it suddenly went very dark. The crowd fell silent and began looking round uneasily. The darkness lasted for three hours, and the victims of the crucifixion weakened visibly. The only sound was the rasping of breath in their lungs as they painfully pushed themselves upwards to be able to breathe, then slumped down again with their weight taken on their arms.

Suddenly, Jesus cried out: 'My God, my God, why have you forsaken me?'

Some of the onlookers thought he was calling for Elijah. One of them soaked a sponge in wine and held it up to Jesus on a long cane, but Jesus turned his head away. Then Jesus gave a loud cry, his head fell forward, and he died.

Conclusion

If the disciples had had a worry monster, it would have been saying all sorts of things. Show a new monster, and this time pin up all the things the disciples would have been worried, scared or afraid of, e.g. I've lost my best friend; God has let me down; I've just wasted three years of my life; I'm going to be killed next. Each worry can be explained as it is pinned up.

It can then be made clear that Christians look on this day with sadness because of everything that Jesus and his friends had to go through, but the difference is that now we know the rest of the story. This day is called Good Friday because it was the day that Good finally beat Evil. Jesus made it clear that his death did not create monsters – it killed them. (*At this point, the disciples' monster can be screwed into a ball and thrown away*)

As well as that, Jesus made it clear that he had beaten all our monsters as well. (*Now screw up and throw away the monster of the children's worries*) Jesus' death was a terrible thing, but out of it came great good.

Prayer

The closing prayer could be along these lines:

> Thank you, God, for taking all our worries away. Thank you for Jesus, for his courage in dying for us and beating all our worry monsters. Thank you for all the great goodness that came out of Jesus' death.

Song: 'Led like a lamb' (SoF 322)

5.3 MARTHA AND MARY

A modern setting of the incident where Martha is angry because her sister Mary prefers to sit and listen to Jesus rather than help prepare the meal. It is based on Luke's version of the story, with the addition of their brother Lazarus from the version in the Fourth Gospel.

Note how in this version of the story, Martha comes alive as a real person and her brother and sister 'see' her for the first time. Note too the way in which 'Laz's friend' is only later revealed as Jesus, although no doubt some children will have guessed.

Song: 'Be still and know that I am God' (HON 52)

Bible reading (based on Luke 10.38-42)

Martha worked in a bank, trying to support her sister Mary (a dreamer who wanted to go to college) and her brother Laz who seemed to spend all his time with some new friends and a preacher. She knew when she got home she would have to cook and clean and pick up after her brother and sister. Laz popped into the bank to say that he'd invited his friend home for a meal that evening. Martha was furious. She finished work, trudged around Sainsbury's buying food to make chicken and vegetables in red wine, a lovely bottle she'd been given for her birthday. She muttered and grumbled all the way home.

When she got home she had to pick Mary's coat and bag up from the hall, no lights were on, no fire lit, and there was Mary miles away, nose in a book, straining to see in the fading light of the window. Mary immediately felt guilty and tried to make amends, but Martha was so grumpy and fussy, as usual.

Martha was working in the kitchen when Laz brought his friend home. Martha could hear

their laughter as she slaved away. 'It's not fair, ever since Mum and Dad died, I've done everything for them and they've taken me for granted and now they've forgotten me,' Martha thought tearfully. She went to the cupboard for the wine. It was gone! Laz had finished it with his friends and not told her or replaced it. It was the last straw; she angrily burst into the living room, where Laz and his friend were sitting by the fire and Mary was sitting by the guest's feet, staring up at him. 'It's not fair!' Martha burst out. 'Mary, come and help me, now. You never help.'

They all turned and looked at her in astonishment – Mary and Laz guiltily and the stranger with very gentle eyes. 'Martha,' the stranger said, getting up and taking her hand, 'don't worry so, come and talk to us, we would love to hear what you've got to say. Laz can go and get fish and chips. Mary will clear away later. Come and sit here.' He continued, 'It's more important to spend time with one another like this than anything else.'

Martha sat and Laz's friend was wonderful to listen to. He was so wise, so gentle, knew so much and he seemed to want to listen to her as well. She poured out her heart, her dreams, her ambitions, her love for God. Mary and Laz were amazed at their sister, how much she knew, her dreams, her thoughts. They felt guilty too. They knew they had not done enough to help her, and resolved to be better in the future. Martha realized that there were more important things than the things she had thought were all-important, fussing around the house, etc. She decided she would spend more time getting to know God.

Leader: This is a story from the Bible, and the stranger is Jesus. Jesus was saying that knowing God is more important than anything else. Sometimes we are like Mary and Laz, making it difficult for others to spend time doing more important things than clearing up after us.

Reflection

Listen to a tape of an instrumental version of 'There is a Redeemer' (HON 500) while reflecting on this.

Prayer

Pray that we may come to know God's love for us.

Alternative version

A simplified version of the above, for Key Stage 1.

All sit quietly and listen to quiet classical music.

The leader lights the candle on the table at the front.

Merit stars are awarded.

Birthday people skip around the room while all sing and clap the birthday song.

The leader then tells a simplified version of the story of Jesus visiting the home of Mary and Martha (see 1.3), embellishing it with domestic details and going on to say that Martha wanted help with all the practical things she did, but Jesus was saying that there are different ways of showing love and care for people, spending time with them, talking and playing with them, helping them with things. Jesus said you can show your love for him by loving others.

The leader asks the children to think how they could show their love to others, while some quiet music is played.

The worship ends with a simple prayer:

> We ask, Father God, that we might all come to know your Son, Jesus Christ's love, in their work and play, at home and at school. Amen.

5.4 HEALING OF THE BLIND MAN

The story of Bartimaeus is introduced by a simple dramatic device to remind us of ways in which people with disabilities such as blindness may need help and also that, despite their disabilities, they may have highly developed skills in other directions – in the case of Bartimaeus, an insight into the power of Jesus and a faith that Jesus could cure him. The miraculous nature of the healing is not emphasized; the emphasis is upon our need to help others, as Jesus helped Bartimaeus, and our need to learn from Bartimaeus.

Introduction

What does the word 'blind' mean? Blindfold a child and then ask if it would be sensible to ask the child to go back to his place on his own without touching anyone or falling over anything. If not, why not?

Get someone else to help the blindfolded child down steps and back to place.

What do people need to help them to see if they are blind? Someone alongside them (blind people in the disabled Olympics used to have someone running alongside tied to their wrist). Sometimes they need us to help them. Sometimes they also have guide dogs for the blind.

Again we are focusing on our need of each other.

Point out that although blind people are physically unable to see, they may sometimes develop other skills; their hearing may become particularly acute, for example, so that they can recognize people coming by the sound of their footsteps.

Bible reading

Tell the story of Bartimaeus recovering his sight (Mark 10.46-52), emphasizing that although he was blind, Bartimaeus had a special insight into Jesus and knew that Jesus could heal him. Because he had faith, Jesus was able to restore his sight. We may not have Jesus' special powers, but we can be ready to help those in need.

Prayer

Pray for those who cannot see the wonderful things we see every day, but who, like Bartimaeus, may be able to see things that we cannot see. Pray that we will always be there to help them when needed. Pray also that we may learn from Bartimaeus the gift of faith.

Song: 'Jesus' hands were kind hands' (JP 134)

5.5 THE DOVE (THE BAPTISM OF JESUS)

A simple cardboard cut-out model is used to symbolize a difficult concept – the Holy Spirit. Making the cardboard wings by cutting out round the outline of a pupil's hand underlines the important message that God gives us his Spirit because he wants to use our hands to work for peace.

Resources: Make a cardboard model of a dove using white body shape and drawing around a pupil's hand to represent wings. The cardboard wings can be fastened to the body by paper fasteners. Green cardboard olive branch.

Bible reading

Leader: We are going to listen to the story of Jesus' Baptism (Matthew 3.13-17) when the Holy Spirit came upon Jesus and it looked like a dove.

Readers: One day, when Jesus was 30 years old, he came out to the wilderness by the River Jordan to see John, his cousin. He asked John to baptize him, but John refused.

'I am the one that ought to be baptized by you,' he said, 'and yet you have come to me!'

'I think it is what God wants,' Jesus said gently.

So John baptized Jesus in the River Jordan. As Jesus came out of the water, he had a vision of the skies opening and God's Spirit coming down to him like a dove.

Children show the cardboard model of the dove.

Reader: Then Jesus heard a voice: 'This is my dear Son, who pleases me very much.'

Leader: This is why the dove is often used as a picture of the Holy Spirit. The

dove is also used as a symbol of peace and so that helps us to remember that the Holy Spirit brings God's peace.

Just before Jesus left his disciples he said that the Holy Spirit would come into them as it had to him. We made the dove with wings made out of the outline of the hands of a child. We want to remember that God gives us his Spirit because he wants to use us to work for peace. We can do that whatever age we are.

Sometimes the dove is seen with an olive branch in its mouth (*stick cardboard olive branch on to dove*). That is because we remember the story of when Noah sent out the dove to look to see if there was any land after the world had been flooded (Genesis 8.8-11). The dove came back with a little branch from an olive tree in its mouth, which showed they were going to be safe.

From these stories we are always reminded by the dove of the love God has for us, wanting us always to be safe and peaceful with him.

Prayer

Thank God for loving us and sending us help when we often need it.

Alternatively, use the prayer of St Teresa of Avila:

> Christ has no body now on earth but yours, no hands but yours, no feet but yours; yours are the eyes through which to look at Christ's compassion to the world, yours are the feet with which he is to go about doing good, and yours are the hands with which he is to bless us now.

(from Christopher Herbert, comp., *Pocket Prayers*, National Society/Church House Publishing, 1994)

Song: 'Let there be peace on earth' (A 42)

5.6 THE TEN LEPERS

Another healing miracle, where once again the emphasis is not upon the miraculous element of the healing – this is taken for granted – but upon the message we can learn from the story, in this case a straightforward moral point. The telling of the story is given a setting by a simple dramatic interlude.

Note The story, in Luke 17.11-19, emphasizes that the one leper who did come back to say thank you to Jesus was a foreigner. The leader of worship, in telling this story, will have to decide whether or not to include this. One way might be to look at the story in the Bible as follow-up in class, with older pupils; this could then be related to a reminder that Luke was writing for Gentiles (non-Jews). Perhaps Luke, in telling this story, was underlining his understanding that the Jews had rejected Jesus, despite what he had done for them, and the gospel was being taken to non-Jews instead.

Preparation Have ready some bags of small (unwrapped) sweets – one bag for each class and one for the staff. Prepare beforehand children to distribute these sweets and to count quietly (in their heads) the number of children who say thank you when given a sweet.

Discussion

Tell the children you have a special treat for them today and ask the children you chose

beforehand to come and give out the treat.

When each child brings the bag back to you, ask 'How many?' and make a big fuss of low or high reported numbers, perhaps writing up the numbers on the board.

Ask the children what they think the monitors are counting.

Story/Playlet

Tell or act out (this could be prepared beforehand) the story of the healing of the ten lepers (Luke 17.11-19). Only one remembered to say thank you. How many of the children remembered to say thank you?

Prayer

> Dear God, please help us always to remember to say thank you when somebody gives us something or does something for us. It is such a little word but it means so much. Don't let us forget it. Amen.

Hymn: 'Thank you Lord for this new day' (C & P 32)

5.7 SHARING (THE FEEDING OF THE 5,000)

Age range: Key Stage 1

A simple act of worship for a Key Stage 1 class assembly. The story and acted-out version of the Feeding of the 5,000 is told simply by the teacher and the sharing of the bread rolls, with everyone just eating a little bit, makes the point graphically that when we share, there is enough to go round.

This could be staged during Christian Aid Week, and the obvious conclusion drawn.

Resources 20 pence in change, two bread rolls, a rug, a picnic basket, paper plates, a purse, Crystal Healing Music by Anthony Miles (New World SKU 345153).

Setting the scene

Play gentle music, if possible with watery, natural sounds, such as crystal healing music. Invite the children to sit in a circle on the floor and light a candle to show it is the beginning of the worship time.

Listen to the music for a few moments. Invite the children to join you at a picnic and spread out the rug in the centre of the circle. Put the picnic basket on the rug and tell the children that you need to prepare everything before you eat. Ask them to pass the paper plates around the circle. Encourage the children to close their eyes and to listen.

Leader: Imagine you are sitting on a grassy hillside near a lake (*listen to the soft music which has watery sounds*); it is a warm, sunny day, feel the warmth of the sun on your face. There are lots of people around you, so many you can't count them. Listen to them chattering; there must be thousands there. Slowly you hear one particular voice, a gentle voice; you look around to see where it is coming from. It is a man, it is Jesus. Jesus

tells everyone about his special home. He tells you all about it and how wonderful it is. You sit there for a long time listening and then you realize that you're hungry, your tummy is rumbling. Open your eyes and see if we can continue with the story.

One of Jesus' friends looks for money to buy some food (*invite a child to take the purse from the basket and count out the money*). Jesus' friends realize that they have very little money and wonder if there will be enough to buy food for everyone there to have a picnic (*discuss with the children whether they think 20 pence will be enough to buy food for everyone there*). Jesus' friends wonder what they are going to do. While they are talking, a little boy comes up to Jesus and offers him his five loaves of bread and two fish from his basket (*remove your two bread rolls from the picnic basket and hold them for everyone to see*). Jesus thanks the little boy but one

of his friends laughs and says it is not enough to feed 5,000 people. Jesus smiles and asks everyone to sit and pray (*invite the children to pray together*).

Father God, please help us to share this food together so that everyone here may have something to eat. Amen.

Jesus then passes the bread and the fish around the crowd of people. Now let us do the same. (*Take a small piece of bread from the roll and pass the rolls in opposite directions around the circle, inviting everyone to share in the food. The children will be surprised to see that there is probably some of the bread left after everyone has eaten*) How do you think Jesus' picnic ended? (*Children give ideas*)

Song: 'Now Jesus one day' (SSL 30)

After singing the song, give the children time for reflection. Ask the children to walk quietly back to their seats.

6 Using children's own poetry

Whenever I visit a primary school, I see delightful examples of children's poetry everywhere – on the walls, in their books, in the Head's study, in the entrance hall. The topics are often very closely related to the experiences of the children: myself; my feelings; growing up; and often about fundamental religious questions, such as belief, life after death, the future of the planet. Yet rarely do I hear these poems read in worship. Why is this? Perhaps because performing poetry is more difficult than writing it? Maybe – but oral skills are just as important as written ones, and performing their own poetry in assembly should be a

good experience for children, both in developing oral skills and in gaining self-confidence. Another reason might be that the poetry was written in the 'English' lesson, not the 'RE' one, and it just didn't occur to the class teacher that work done in English would be appropriate for celebration in collective worship.

The examples which follow are of acts of worship which use poems by children, all at Key Stage 2. The poems are, I think, typical of work that OFSTED, in their dour, unenthusiastic way, would probably deem 'sound' or 'satis-factory'; they are certainly not exceptional and, if on reading them, your response is,

'Well, my children write better poetry than that!' then I would say, 'Three cheers!' and suggest you use your children's poetry in worship. It is certainly not the intention that these examples of acts of worship should be repeated in schools up and down the country; rather that teachers should be encouraged, by reading them, to compile their own acts of worship using poetry written by children in their class or school.

6.1 FEELINGS

This is an act of worship based on poetry about feelings, written by children. One way of stimulating poetry about, for example, happiness, would be to make a taped collection of sounds that make you happy. They may be sounds that are associated with things you like (the rustle of paper as you unwrap a present) or that seem to be happy to you (recordings of happy poems, happy sayings, a group of people being happy, laughing) or just a tune that makes you happy. By tape editing try to make a sound scrapbook of class happiness. You could even try recording some of the sounds simultaneously (laughing, dancing or a tune behind one of the poems?). This tape could then also be used in the worship.

Introductory music: Play some music which has a strong sentiment of happiness, such as 'These are a few of my favourite things' from *The Sound of Music*.

Poems

Ask the children how this music makes them feel; hopefully the word 'happy' will be among the responses! Introduce the children who are going to read their poems: 'The children from class —— have been writing some poems about happiness.' Children then read their poem. Here are just three examples:

Happiness

Happiness is when I see both my nans
Happiness is when I come to school
Happiness is when my puppy comes
    home
Happiness is when it is Friday
Happiness is when I do the washing up
Happiness is when I get a pet rat
Happiness is when my mum fetches
    me from school.

(Chloe Talbot, age 9)

Happiness

Happiness is McManaman scoring a
    hattrick.
Happiness is going to my Nan's for
    tea.
Happiness is getting pocket money.
Happiness is watching the Simpsons.
Happiness is getting a new watch.
Happiness is being the bell monitor.
Happiness is Christmas.
Happiness is being happy.

(Adam Massam, age 10)

A good time

A good time is playing with mates.
A good time is peacefully fishing.
A good time is plaice, crab and dab
    lining.
A good time is chugging along in our
    boat.
A good time is remembering you've
    got six weeks' holiday.
A good time is canoeing with
    Michael.
A good time is doing Jazzamatazz
    with Mrs Sheppard.

(Samuel Garth, age 10)

Play the tape of sounds that make people happy, and ask the children to try and identify them. Then, time permitting, ask the children present to say some of the things that make them happy.

Then say that, of course, we're not happy all the time. Play some particularly sad and gloomy music, such as 'Valse Triste' (Sibelius) or 'Ole Man River' (from *Showboat*). How does this make the children feel?

Then more children read their own poems, such as the following:

Sadness

Sadness is when Princess Diana died.
Sadness is when your brother or sister
is getting told off.
Sadness is when someone you care
about has been hurt really badly.
Sadness is when you ask for a friend
round and your mum says no.

(Paula East, age 11)

Anger

Anger is when we break down.
Anger is when the theme park is
closed.
Anger is being blamed for something
I didn't do.
Anger is when the cat leaves black
footprints all over my bed.

(Ben Fensom, age 10)

Disappointment

Disappointment is the electricity going
off.
Disappointment is when the tea gets
burnt.
Disappointment is getting a present
that's broken.
Disappointment is when you get 9 out
of 10 in spellings.
Disappointment is the cake going stale.
Disappointment is buying something
to eat that's out of date.

(Adam Pilgrim, age 9)

Explain that we will all experience times of happiness, and times of unhappiness. For example, when Peter had a flash of insight and realized that Jesus was the Christ, the Saviour that the Jews had been waiting for, he was commended by Jesus (Matthew 16.15-17).

Bible reading

Readers: Jesus and the disciples went north to the town of Caesarea Philippi, on the southern slopes of Mount Hermon.

'Tell me,' Jesus said to them as they were walking along, 'who do people say that I am?'

'Some say you are John the Baptist,' they replied. 'Others think you are Elijah, or another of the prophets come back again.'

'And what about you?' asked Jesus. 'Who do you think I am?'

Peter was the one to reply. 'I think that you are the Messiah,' he said. 'You are right,' Jesus replied.

Leader: This must have made Peter feel very happy. But later, when Jesus was being tried by the High Priest, Peter was scared and denied he had ever known Jesus (Matthew 26. 73-75):

Readers: Meanwhile, Peter was still waiting in the courtyard. A serving maid came up and looked at him curiously.

'Weren't you one of the followers of Jesus?' she asked.

'I don't know what you're talking about,' Peter said. He went out to the porch, but the serving maid began pointing him out to the men in the yard, saying he was one of the men who had been with Jesus. Again Peter denied it.

One of the men came over to Peter.

'I reckon you are a follower of Jesus, you know,' he said. 'Your Galilean accent gives you away.'

Peter cursed, and swore that he didn't even know Jesus. Then he heard the cock crow, and remembered what Jesus had said. He ran out, weeping bitterly.

Leader: When he realized what he'd done, Peter must have been desperately unhappy.

Sad times, happy times; we are bound to experience both in our lifetime. Whether we are sad or happy, God loves us and shares our feelings.

Song: 'To everything, turn, turn, turn' (C & P 113)

Prayer

Thank you, God, for happy times, and help us to manage when we feel unhappy. Help us to know that you are with us at all times. Amen.

Exit music: Go out to 'happy' music.

6.2 CHANGES THROUGH LIFE

This act of worship uses poems written by children about themselves: how they change as they grow up; how people change as they journey through life; and how the essential 'me' stays the same.

Opening music: 'Yellow submarine' (Lennon & McCartney) or Honegger: Three Symphonic Movements No. 1, 'Pacific 231' (an orchestral piece, describing the journey of a railway engine).

Leader: Today we are going to think about ourselves and our journey through life.

Hymn: 'Travel on' (C & P 42)

Poems

Leader: Boys and girls from ____ class have been thinking about how people change as they travel through life, and they have written some poems about this.

Changes through life

When I was a baby
I slept in a cot,
10 and 20ps
I was spoilt a lot.

Next a toddler
A new bed I got,
Sticking biscuits under cushions,
Waiting to rot.

Now I am a Junior
Learning to write,
Some people say
I'm really very bright.

When I am a teenager
Going to the pub.
Cruising in my motorcar
Visiting the nightclub.

When I'm in my 20s
Move out, be free,
I may live
In luxury.

Then I am 50
With slower hobbies
No more running into
Police bobbies.

When I am old
Sitting in my chair
Just watching the TV
With my grey hair.

(Trevor Payne, age 10)

Changes through life

Crying and crawling, throwing food,
That's the thing that babies do.
Always needing help from dad and
    mum,
Can't do anything but suck its thumb.

Then the toddler starts to walk,
In their own language they start to
    talk.
Always amusing themselves with
    books and toys,
Tantrums in all girls and boys!

The junior starts primary school,
Starts hobbies like going to the swim-
    ming pool.
Begin to learn to read and write,
Hopefully never learn to fight!

Teenagers do exams at school,
With mum and dad they start a duel!
All that matters is clothes and shops,
The interest in fashion never stops!

In their 20s and 30s the men get a
    wife,
To live with for the rest of their life.
Get a job and get a car,
Have children and start travelling afar.

In the 40s and 50s they start losing
    hair,
Or it starts going grey; the head looks
    quite bare.
They say that they are very wise,
Who knows if they are all lies?

Slowing down, getting frail.
Can't go out in snow or hail.
Wrinkled and retired, so is his wife!
The last part of their long life.

(Jodie Bradshaw, age 10)

Changes through life

Changes through life
Crying and dribbling,
All through the night
Sucking their thumbs,
With delight.
Then comes the toddler,
Tantrums galore,
'Please,' said the mum,
'No more! No More!'
They're now going to primary school,
Relief for the mum,
Then comes the question,
'Can Laura come?'
Now comes the teenager,
The war starts.
Battle stations please,
Here they come, her and Louise,
They're now in their 20s
Their careers begin
Driving fast cars and drinking gin.
They are older now
Weaker but wiser
They still like to travel

But only in a cruiser.
Older and thinner
Staying at home,
Watching children passing by,
Beginning to die.

(Nastassja Beaton, age 10)

Leader: Yes, we are all changing as we grow up and develop, first into teenagers, then into grown-ups; but the real 'me', the person inside, somehow stays the same person, even though all the experiences of the journey of life cause us to grow and develop. What is the real 'me'? Here are some poems which explore the 'inside person':

Myself

I have big green eyes and pointed
   ears,
I'm never told off for telling lies.
But can easily be seen with tears.

My computer amuses me,
I love to eat tomatoes for my tea,
My favourite football team is Leeds
I also enjoy eating peas.

Painting is one of my hobbies,
Colouring red all of the poppies,
I don't like moody brothers,
But I have a lovely mother.

I don't like crusts and brown bread
Or having to go early to bed.

(Jay Wyatt, age 8)

Myself

I have brown eyes and hair
I try not to stare
I'm not very broad
My name is often called.

I don't like oranges
Nor Beecham's lozenges
I quite like apples
And go to St John's chapel.

I don't like to cook
Or read my book.
I passed my 11-plus
And go to town on the bus.

My hobby is drawing
It never gets boring
I want to be a pilot
And like the colour violet.

(Lee Hunt, age 10)

Leader: So you see, it's not just what we look like that makes us what we are, it's much more than that. It's the things we like doing, the people who love us and care for us like our mothers or nans, and all our hopes and ambitions for what we might become. Christians believe that all through the journey of life, not only do we have our family and friends to support us, we also have Jesus Christ at our side to keep us on the right path.

Song: 'The journey of life' (C & P 45)

Prayer

Dear Lord Jesus, help us on our journey through life to follow in your footsteps, to do the right things and to make the right choices. Stay by our side whether the journey is easy or hard, and help us to find our way to be with you. Amen.

6.3 ANCIENT EGYPT AND THE TOMB OF TUTANKHAMUN

This act of worship makes use of creative work by pupils written as part of National Curriculum History.

Resources Posters of Great Pyramid and Tutankhamen.

Introductory music: 'Gloria all'Egitto' from *Aida* (Verdi).

Leader: Class —— have been learning all about ancient Egypt, and in particular, why they built amazing buildings like these (*display poster showing the Great Pyramid*).

Do you know what this is?

That's right – it's a pyramid. But do you know what it was for? (*Draw out answer that it was a tomb – a place where a dead person was buried*)

What sort of person would have been buried in an enormous building like this?

Yes – a very important person – probably a king, or a pharaoh as they were called in Egypt. The body of the king would be placed

with great care and respect inside a beautifully carved box called a sarcophagus, and this was covered by a magnificent representation of what the king would have looked like during his lifetime. One of these was a king called Tutankhamun (*show poster of Tutankhamun*).

We don't know exactly why the ancient Egyptians took so much trouble over the burial of their dead kings, but we think it had something to do with their belief in life after death. It's as if the dead king was being prepared to enter the after-life with as much wealth and splendour as possible.

The pyramids stood, silent and deserted, long after the fall of ancient Egypt, in the lonely, windswept sands of the desert. Sometimes robbers managed to break in and steal some of the gold and precious objects placed with the bodies of the ancient pharaohs; but only in recent times have archaeologists managed to make a proper study of the contents of the pyramids, to help us to learn about this ancient civilization.

The boys and girls of class —— have written some poems about the discovery of the tomb of Tutankhamun.

Egypt

Tutankhamun one of the kings
He was found with many things.
All the treasures covered in gold
They were ever ever so old.
A dagger covered in gold
Could it have been four thousand
   years old?
A vulture necklace wings abreast
But of the treasures it is not the best.

Senet was an ancient game
With a very funny name.
The ancient Egyptians used to pre-
    sume
That if they put models in your tomb
They would come alive
And help you in your next life.

(Adam Pilgrim, age 9)

Ancient Egypt

The Jackal is the God of the Dead
He wraps up the body, feet and head.
They put the mummy in a sarcophagus
And put him in the tomb,
The robbers broke into most of them –
but didn't find Tutankhamun.
One day a boy found a flight of steps.
They led to a secret door
They made a little hole in it –
and saw treasures that covered the
    floor!

(Andrew Iszatt, age 9)

The tomb of Tutankhamun

We walked down the stairs in the
    misty light
And I looked through the hole with a
    candle light
All that glistening shining gold
This was a tale that had to be told
As we entered the dark gloomy room
All I could see were wonderful things
Like diamonds, jewels and golden
    rings
Everything you could wish
There were even statues of guard
    dogs and pythons
Still waiting and guarding the room
But wait a minute where was the
    tomb?
We turned around and there it was
We opened the tombs
And unwrapped them
And there he was, Tutankhamun
    himself.

(Rebecca Pailing, age 10)

Leader: We don't have any Egyptian hymns or songs to sing, so instead we're going to sing a song about the desert.

Song: 'Desert Rain' ('The sun burns hot') (C & P 77)

Prayer

Help us to learn more and more about other civilizations and their beliefs. Just as the people of ancient Egypt thought about life after death and prepared for it carefully, help us to remember that everybody will have to die some-day, and to think about the meaning of life on earth. We pray for anybody we knew and loved who has died, and we commend their souls to the love of God, just as the ancient Egyptians commended their loved and respected kings to the after-life that they believed in. Amen.

Going-out music: *Aida* (Verdi).

6.4 SAVE OUR PLANET!

This act of worship starts with one of the many famous photographs of the earth seen from the moon, as a ball travelling through space, and uses poetry to express ecological concern for our future survival.

Resources Large poster with photograph of earth from space.

Opening music: Holst, *The Planets Suite*: 'Uranus the Magician' (the Magician seems to be defeated by his own spells, with the huge shattering glissando near the end).

Leader: When we walk about day by day, doing all the everyday things we all do, like having our breakfast, coming to school, going out to play, it's very easy to forget that we are standing on a planet that is hurtling through space at hundreds of miles per hour and that we depend for our survival on a complex blend of sunshine and rain to make the crops grow, air to breathe and a mysterious force called gravity that holds it all together. The photographs of the earth from outer space remind us just how fragile this system is (*show large photograph of earth seen from space*).

Boys and girls from —— class have been thinking about the beauty of the earth as it spins through space.

Poem

The world

The world is a ball in space
The world is a circle of beauty
The world is a caring mother
The world is a land of adventure
The world is a God of glory.

(Danielle Clark, age 10)

Leader: They have also been asking themselves some questions about the future of planet Earth, this 'ball in space' that we live on. It's wonderful that we can travel to the moon and perhaps one day will be able to travel to other planets, but that's no good if we let our own planet be killed off by pollution, our wildlife be destroyed by greedy hunters and the rainforest that gives us oxygen to breathe be cut down for short-term profit. Here are some of their concerns, expressed in poetry.

Cosmic poem

Would you rather go to space
Or try and help our human race?
People talk about going to the moon.
They don't really care if our planet is doomed.

Space can wait its turn
Planet Earth is my concern.
While you're digging on Mars with a spade
Can't you stop the wicked fur trade?

(Mark Smith, age 10)

Cosmic Poem

It's very well that we are heading to the stars,
And will soon land chaps upon Mars.
But before we think of outer space,
We should think about our place.
So it's time if we're fit,
To tidy up our Earth a bit.
Oil-filled seas,
Flooding up to our knees.
Ivory tusks, the fur trade and more,
We can't even care for the poor.
The rainforest is being cut down,
Watch trees fall to the ground.
Child abuse is increasing,
While the countryside is decreasing.
So before you think of Outer Space,
Think about the Human Race.

(Matthew Green, age 10)

Save our planet

Think of our planet and what we've
    done
Instead of thinking about aliens, chum
Go back to the people who are feel-
    ing sick
Our Earth's in danger so look after it,
Quick
The animals are dying because of our
    testing
Why don't we start suggesting
Forget about that other world
Save our animals and save our world!

(Rebecca Pailing, age 10)

Save our earth!

I protest against the fur coats,
But ivory is what I hate most.
People talk about landing on the
    moon,
And don't really care if our planet is
    doomed.
Nuclear bombs give us no choice,
Next we know we will have no voice,
Waiting for the Earth to withdraw,
Go; open the Earth's door.
We will never have another chance
This planet we will have to enhance.

(Hayley Collins, age 10)

Leader: Our readers have reminded us how important it is that we should all be concerned to help preserve the planet Earth, which is our home. We are going to sing a hymn that reminds us how awful the world would be without flowers and trees, without animals, fish, and birds – and without people.

Song: 'Think of a world without any flowers' (C & P 17)

Leader: We have thanked God in our hymn, for flowers and trees and sunshine; for all God's living crea-

tures; and for families and friend-ship. Now we are going to have a final poem, which is a prayer of praise to God.

Prayer

Praise God for the beauty of the skies,
Praise God for the clouds that pass by.
You filled the oceans with your crea-
    tures,
You filled the Earth with different fea-
    tures.
The heavens shout that God is great.
You opened up the heavenly gate.

(Georgina Workman, age 10)

Going-out music: Wagner, *Twilight of the Gods*: the 'Magic Fire' music.

6.5 WINTER

An act of worship which was one of a series on creation, but which can equally well stand alone. The intention is to draw children's attention to the beauty of winter, and its place in the pattern of seasonal change.

Introductory music: Vivaldi, *The Four Seasons*, 'Winter'.

Ask children to tell you what they know about winter: cold, can be dark, sometimes there's snow, etc.

Poems

These two examples are by Year 6 pupils.

Seasons

Winter's a white, cold, dragon
with breath of freezing ice.
Travelling here and there like a
    wagon,
and certainly not very nice.

Following winter the lady of spring,
who in her power captures pain.
She again brings
songs and dance after the dragon's
    reign.

Summer soon follows a maid of
    colours,
bright in bloom shining like a pin.
Though soon summer colours are
    duller
and summer fades as autumn rolls in.

Autumn colours are cloaked around
as the window of winter mellows in age.
She sinks in the cold, wet ground
as she takes her leave of life's stage.

(Samantha Elliott)

Winter's dawn

Look outside on winter's morning,
the ground as white as a thick cloud.
Rainy snowflakes flopping onto the
    ground,
look around, look around, look
    around.

The snow lays like layered cotton wool,
and the ice as clear as glass.
Witty little children up and awake,
near the lake, near the lake, near the
    lake.

You hurry outside as fast as you can
shouting like an angry giant.
Running past the tied-up hay
stay away, stay away, stay away.

They hear you and turn
they look as pale as a ghost.
You see they're sleepwalking
but no talking, no talking, no talking.

You take them home to their beds
you are breathing like a run-out horse.
Then to you it's clear
winter's here, winter's here, winter's
    here.

(Peter Buckley)

Reflection

The beauty of nature, lying dormant (sleeping) at wintertime; features of cold weather: ice, snow, frost; the fun we have in the snow; the dangers of cold weather: darkness, slippery ice. The expectation of new life in the spring.

Song: 'Lay my white cloak' (C & P 112)

Going-out music: *The Four Seasons.*

7 Different approaches to prayer

Many people give up on prayer because they were taught, or they somehow got the impression, that prayer is all about asking God to do something for you. They've tried it and it didn't work; Grannie didn't get better, Dad didn't come home, their team didn't win the cup, so clearly prayer is a waste of time and God doesn't exist. Let's start again!

First of all, prayer is a two-way process. Yes, it is about expressing our thoughts to God; but more importantly, it's about laying ourselves open for God to speak to us. This is the bit we've tended not to teach, perhaps because it's too difficult, perhaps because many adults themselves are unsure about this dimension of prayer.

So, because it must be the more important of the two sides to prayer, let's start with the 'God speaking to us' dimension. It's a bit scary, if it really happens; the story of the child Samuel in the temple springs to mind, with the mysterious voice calling the child's name . . . surely that isn't what we're looking for? I think not – not unless we have some prophetic prodigies on the school roll. A better analogy would be spiritual development. We don't really know how spiritual development happens, we just know there are certain environments in which children are more likely to develop spiritually, such as homes and schools where a spiritual dimension is taken for granted, when God is assumed to be real and is spoken about naturally, where people's actions are consistent with their expressed beliefs, and where love and forgiveness are experienced day by day.

The kind of worship, then, in which we and the children might experience God 'speaking' to us, is going to be worship where we take it for granted that God will speak to us and regularly allow time for this to happen. This means moments of silence following some kind of input to give us something to reflect upon. You will find examples of this in the acts of worship which follow.

Another way in which God speaks to us, of course, is through the Bible, and there are many examples in other chapters of creative ways of making the Bible come alive.

A third way in which God speaks to us is through other people. The Jewish philosopher Martin Buber wrote: 'Through every other "thou" one catches a glimpse of the eternal "Thou".'

It is a frightening thought, but we as responsible adults are not merely role models for the children in our charge but also in a real sense the mirrors in which children see the loving, caring, forgiving and accepting nature of God. If we're serious about giving the children an experience of a genuine, loving Christian community, which, particularly in a church school, we have to be, this is an issue we cannot duck. It's no good saying, like Moses, 'Oh Lord, I'm just not a good speaker' – we know what God's reply will be (Exodus 4.11-12, if you're not quite sure).

And the 'speaking to God' aspect of prayer? It's a lot easier than you think. Don't make a mystery of it with all that 'Adoration – Confession – Thanksgiving – Supplication' stuff that you and I had at Sunday school when we were kids. Just think about the theme of the act of worship and talk to God about it, easily and naturally in ordinary everyday language. Encourage children to write and read out their own prayers. (But perhaps edit them before they're read out; an act of worship I attended recently on Passover included one child's prayer, 'Thank

you, God, for killing all the Egyptian soldiers' – which might have been better omitted!)

Another very helpful approach to prayer, which involves everyone present, is the 'versicles and responses' format, in which a line spoken by the leader of worship is responded to by the congregation. This has a long and honoured tradition in the Anglican liturgy. Worship in church schools is, of course, supposed to be 'in accordance with the school's Trust Deed', which in theory would allow Anglican schools to introduce children to Matins and Evensong, and traditional versicles and responses such as:

> **Minister:** Show us your mercy, O Lord;
> **People:** And grant us your salvation.

> (from Morning Prayer,
> *The Alternative Service Book* 1980)

But even this 1980 version has difficult language; 'salvation' is a hard concept for Key Stage 1! The format is, however, a very good way of involving everyone present in the worship, and once the 'people' are familiar with what is expected, they usually join in with enthusiasm. (One only has to think of when Bruce Forsyth was on The Generation Game: **Bruce:** Nice to see you; **Audience:** To see you – nice!)

Using this style of formal worship in collective worship in school can also be a useful introduction to aspects of the liturgy of the Holy Communion, such as:

> **Priest:** The Lord be with you;
> **People:** And also with you.

Come to think of it, that's not too difficult as it stands! Why don't we use it in school?

Note See also the notes about using prayers from other traditions, Chapter 9.

7.1 PEACE

The act of worship focuses around the theme of peace. Children are given the opportunity to explore various kinds of peace and then to reflect on their thoughts. The visual stimulus that the peace river pro-

vides enables all contributions to the worship to be valued. Candles reflect the five areas of peace that have been explored. A central candle used for daily worship is also present; above it hangs a simple cross.

Resources A length of blue material which is gently moved to create a peace river. Cards with the word 'Peace' written on them. Five small candles that can be held by children. Main candle which is alight at the start of this act.

Entry music: 'Strange how my heart' (from *Shepherd's Moon* by Enya, WEA Records, 9031-75572-2).

Entry: As children and staff enter the hall the Enya music is quietly playing. Two children are already in place and moving the peace river from side to side to create ripples.

Introduction

Tell the children that today we are going to explore the meaning of 'peace'. What does peace mean? Peace may be lying on a bed, it may be the end of war, it may be stillness. As the children give you ideas and peace statements, invite them to collect a card and gently place it or pin it on the river. Collect about 30 contributions in all; they may be words, things, times or phrases. After the final card has been placed on the river, add one more as a way of acknowledging the thoughts of others who have not responded.

Song: 'Peace is flowing like a river' (C & P 144)

Thank the children and staff for their thoughts and start to talk about the kinds of peace that they have mentioned so that the following categories emerge. Invite further contributions from the children. At the end of each section light a candle symbolizing that kind of peace and ask a child to hold it. It is a good idea to use a disc of cardboard with a hole in the centre to hold the candle, to prevent problems with dripping wax.

What follows is an example of how this developed in one school; the response may of course vary from school to school depending on the contributions from the children.

Peace amongst nations

wars to cease
fighting to stop
harmony and understanding
media coverage of destruction and
    desolation
wanting things to be right

Peace amongst communities

areas where people are scared to go
    out
areas of racial tension
care facilities offered
pleasant places for all to live
keeping laws and rules
care for the elderly
good neighbours
wanting things to be right

Peace amongst ourselves

being understanding
friendships
care within our school
getting things right between ourselves
thinking of others' feelings
times of stillness
wanting things to be right

Inner peace

times to reflect, music, art
meditation
lying on your bed
being asleep
feeling comfortable with yourself
unstressed
wanting things to be right

Peace with God

through prayer
letting God into our lives
being open to what he says
by believing he is around us
wanting things to be right

Song: 'Spirit of peace' (C & P 85)

Prayer

Let us pray and be still. Many people think that peace only means that there is no fighting going on. Christians believe peace is much more than that. It is when everything is right between people. You might not be fighting with your friend, but you might be sulking. That would not be peaceful in the way the Bible means.

> Lord we pray for peace when everything is right between people.

(Short period of silence)

Song: 'Na jijoho, Peace be with you' (WP)

Prayer

> Lord we think of our five candles.
> We pray for peace amongst nations
> Peace in our community
> Peace amongst ourselves
> Inner peace
> Peace with you, our God.

(Short period of silence)

Song: 'Na jijoho, Peace be with you'

Prayer

> We thank you for the life of Jesus who came to put things right, to bring real peace, Jesus 'the Prince of Peace'.

Song: 'Na jijoho, Peace be with you'

Leader: We lit our five candles from the main candle. The main candle reminds us of God's presence here. Today we are reminded that peace is a God-given gift. Above our candle is the cross that reminds us of Jesus. Jesus 'the Prince of Peace' came to spread peace over the land.

Reflection

The peace river starts to flow and Enya music is repeated. Thank the children for their thoughts and contributions. As they look at the river ask them to think about the statements and the candles that have been lit. Remind them that peace can flow freely like our river but that it doesn't happen naturally – people have to work for peace.

7.2 EYES TO SEE

A celebration of what eyes are for, using the simple resource of a collection of objects of different sizes, shapes and colours. The prayer is in the form of a litany. It is, of course, very important to be sensitive if there are children who are partially sighted.

Resources A number of objects of different shapes and colours and a box.

Introduction

Show the different objects to the children and put them on display. Ask them their five most favourite sights.

Bible reading

The Lord has given us eyes to see (Proverbs 20.12).

Leader: God has filled the world with beautiful things to see. He could have made it dull and boring. He could have made everything the same shape and colour instead of giving us lots of different shapes and colours. Imagine a square sun and rectangular mountains!

Using the objects, talk about all the different shapes and colours in the world. God has given us millions of different shapes and colours. He is an extravagant God!

God also gave us eyes to notice things – when people are happy or sad, when people need help, e.g. Grandma loses glasses and child helps look for them, etc.

Ask the children to close their eyes and think of some of the colours there are – their favourite colours.

Prayer

Thank God for eyes to see and for colours and shapes. Children can respond with 'We thank you, Lord.'

A simple litany, which can vary depending on the objects that have been displayed or the school setting, might be something like this:

> We thank God for all the beautiful things we see around us – the hills, the trees, the rivers, the sky, the clouds, the houses and streets and shops and factories; *We thank you, Lord.*
>
> We thank God for colour: for brightly painted rooms, for clothes and ribbons and pictures, for team colours and flags, for school uniforms and leisure clothes, for party dresses and shirts; *We thank you, Lord.*
>
> We thank God for light: for sunlight and moonlight, for stars, for streetlights and torchlight, for car

headlights and bicycle lamps, for warning lights and Christmas tree lights, and for the beauty of the rainbow; *We thank you, Lord.*

We thank God for shape and size, for shiny objects and dull ones, for misty distant views and clear, sharp frosty mornings, for hazy, hot summer days and cloudy, foggy autumn mornings, and for all the interest and variety of the visual world he has created; *We thank you, Lord.*

We thank God for the gift of sight, for eyes to see and minds to marvel. We pray for all those who are blind or partially sighted, and for those who work for them – the doctors, the nurses, the research scientists, the friends and helpers who contribute to making their lives rich and full, even in the absence of the gift of sight; *We thank you, Lord.*

Song: 'Give us eyes Lord' (SSL 18)

7.3 A SERVICE OF THANKSGIVING FOR OUR SCHOOL

This is a special service for the twenty-fifth anniversary of the school building, but could obviously be adapted for any anniversary. It contains two types of prayer: an 'encircling' prayer from Iona, using candles and music; and a traditional prayer, addressed to Jesus, 'My Best Friend'.

Setting The local parish church.

Song: 'In the Lord I'll be ever thankful' (HON 250)

The first day

The first day: Memories of a previous headteacher. A short talk by a previous headteacher of the school (if available!).

Song: 'As the deer pants for the water' (MP 37)

The first day for a child in the 1970s: A parent talks about her memories of her first day at the school, twenty-five years ago.

The first day for a child nowadays: Some Year One children each say a sentence about their first day at school.

Song: 'Father in my life' (CH 452)

Prayer

Encircling prayer: 'I will light a light' (see 4.4, page 37) – spoken with musical accompaniment and lighting of candles ('Within our darkest night', HON 562).

Song: 'Be still, for the presence of the Lord' (MP 50)

Prayer

Use the words of the song 'Jesus, friend of little children' as a basis for prayer (S & P 363).

Song: 'How lovely on the mountains' (MP 249)

7.4 COMMUNICATING

This act of worship aims to illustrate how all over the world, and particularly in Africa where Christianity is the fastest growing religion, people use music to express praise and worship. It also uses prayer in the form of a letter to God, written by the children.

Introductory music: (*played when the children are settled, not as entry music*) 'Inkanyezi Nezazi' ('The star and the wiseman' by Ladysmith Black Mombazo –

probably known to the children as a Heinz soup commercial) from *Heavenly* (Gallo Music International, South Africa, 1997).

Ask children how that music makes them feel.

Read the dedication from the *Heavenly* CD cover (a dedication to God, his children everywhere and the joy this music brings because it is a form of praise).

Song: 'All over the world' (MP 18)

Prayer

We are all part of God's family. We can talk to God through music and speech. This letter to God was written by Year 6 pupils:

Dear Father God, we have just listened to some brill music by an African band who were singing to you, so we expect you heard it too. It made us feel very happy because it was the same as the advert for soup. Some of us joined in.

Thank you for voices to sing and speak with, friends to join in with, musicians to lead us. Thank you that you enjoy hearing us and we enjoy praising you.

We think of all the people in Africa and around the world who suffer because they have not got enough food, drink or money. We are thinking of the boys and girls we write to and hope they like the presents we sent them.

We are very busy in school and everyone is working hard. Please help us all to do our best and remember to be considerate to each other.

Please enjoy the music again. We will talk to you again very soon. Love, our school.

Going-out music: Further music from the album *Heavenly*.

8 Using children's creative written work

Most primary schools are very good at stimulating creative written work in the classroom, but few seem to use the end product as a basis for worship. This may be because we have in the past tended to think of worship as a 'religious' activity, in the narrow sense of the word, i.e. restricted to overtly religious topics such as God and Jesus, with traditional hymns and prayers couched in rather old-fashioned, formal language. (Some OFSTED advice to Inspectors, telling them what to look for in collective worship, seems to reinforce this image of worship. Don't be afraid to open the Inspectors' eyes to what worship can be like; Inspectors can learn too.)

Let the starting point for our worship in school be the genuine concerns of our community – the hopes and fears of children growing up in a world which can sometimes be frightening and hostile; our feelings of joy and happiness, of thankfulness and celebration, of sadness and sometimes despair; our experiences of friendship and love, of loneliness and fear, of excitement and anticipation, sometimes of boredom or anxiety. If worship is to be real, it must start from real experiences – just as creative written work, even if it grows and flowers through the stimulus of the imagination, must take as its starting point the genuine experience of the writer. It would seem not only natural but appropriate for creative work of this kind to be used in worship.

There are a number of practical advantages in using children's work in worship in this way. It shows them that their work is valued; we are saying, 'This is of worth' (which, going back to Anglo-Saxon roots, is what worship means). It is a way of celebrating the curriculum and underlining the importance of the written word. It allows an opportunity for children to practise their reading skills in front of an audience. But above all, as the examples which follow demonstrate, children's own writing can be a powerful stimulus to reflection and prayer.

8.1 LOVE

Prior to the act of worship, the teacher discussed the nature of love with a Year Four class, and asked them to write down their ideas about love. Some of these were selected to be read in the act of worship.

Resources Cardboard cut-out tree with apples, the apples representing the fruits of friendship with God; twig – bare; selection of children's writing about love.

Introduction

The assembly begins with the leader showing the children a bare twig from a tree. She asks the children what is hidden deep inside the twig.

The pupils are able to say that inside what appears to be a dead piece of wood is sap – the hidden inner life of the tree. What is hidden deep inside us? Our thoughts – our spirit – our inner life. With the tree and the twig, each have sap which gives the tree life to create fruits – fruits which could give new trees life. We can see the fruits.

What shows the inner life in us? How can we tell what a person is like or what they are thinking? Our actions? Our facial expressions? What we say and do?

The leader then directs the children's attention to the large cut-out tree. She turns an apple over to reveal the word 'love'.

Leader: What is love? How can we show love? Can we see it? I love chocolate. I love swimming. I love walking by the sea. Are these types of love all the same? Perhaps we could put in other words instead of 'love', like 'enjoy' or 'take pleasure from'.

Bible reading

1 Corinthians 13.1-7; Paul considers love:

Now I will show you the best way to live. I may speak like an angel, but if I have no love, I will sound like the clatter of a dustbin lid.

I may have the gift of second sight, and be able to foretell the future; but without love, I am useless.

Love is patient; love is kind, and doesn't envy anyone. Love is not boastful or rude, nor is it easily offended. Love does not nurse grievances or gloat over other people's misfortunes. There is nothing love cannot face up to.

Prophecies, visions, knowledge . . . all these are partial, and will fade away. There are three things that will last for ever – faith, hope and love. But of these, the greatest is love.

Leader: Are we any nearer to knowing what love is and how we can show it?

Song: 'Jubilate' (JP 145)

Class readings

Personal views of what love is.

What is love?

Love is a presence. It is not matter or antimatter. It is a feeling inside you. Love is a never ending circle. Inescapable. Love can be deep down or on the surface. It can be expressed through a hug or a kiss. Feeling love is like feeling pure joy. Love is like a join between two people.

Love

Love is . . . warm and caring.
Love is . . . happiness and giving.
Love is . . . kind and soft.
Love is . . . heartbeating.
Love is . . . like a string of friendship bound together which can never break.

Love is

I get the feeling inside me that as I get older I get more loving and love a lot more things. I loved it when my brother Craig was born. I just couldn't stop looking at him. He was so lovely. I just felt the love growing inside me. I didn't like it when Craig broke his arm. I just wanted to be with him because I loved him. My love sank when he went to a friend's house and he was late back because a road was closed off. I was worried and anxious. I think love is when you have got a feeling inside you. You might feel the pain as you are growing older.

Love is

I think love is a power we use on people whom we like a lot. Love varies everything really, not just one thing. Love feels good. It sometimes gets lost in your heart. Some people don't want love because they might have had it before but then it broke so they don't want that to happen again. You can't see love but you can feel it inside. Sometimes I say horrible things to my brothers like 'I hate you,' but I don't mean it inside. I worry about them. My mum and dad show love by hugging me and kissing me. That is a sign of love. Love is not a present that you can pick up; you have to work for it. It is very colourful and is like a never-ending friendship. When my cousin was born I was really happy. My love inside was growing and growing every time I saw him. God is a power of love. His love will never end. My family's love will never end to me.

Love is

Love can have two meanings. It can mean 'I love such and such because they look cute' or it can mean 'I love apples and pears'. Love is something like the wind because you can't see it but you can feel it against you. When you're in love it is like having a really close friend. Love is red and pink. It's not blue or green. People who have not got love feel really lonely because not everyone has love. It is hard to show at first but then it becomes clearer. Love is like music because it flows all over the world. You can't pick love up but you can feel it.

Love is

Love is when people take time to listen and understand.
Love is when people stay by your side even if you were wrong.
Love is something you can't see but you can feel it all the time, even when you are arguing. When I fall out with my mum I feel all bad inside afterwards and the only thing I can do is to give her a hug.

Love is not

When you don't care.
When you hate someone.
When you say horrible things.
When you make someone's heart sink.
Love isn't hitting.
Love isn't when you take the micky when someone is trying to learn.
Love isn't thinking you can do better.
Love isn't writing bad things about people or shouting at people for nothing.

Love isn't . . .

Hitting someone,
Having a weight on your back.
Laughing at someone for doing a mistake and saying, 'I could do better than that', just because you're jealous.

Love in the Bible

Ruth in the Bible went with Naomi, her mother-in-law, even though she didn't know anyone in the place they were going to. She was going to leave her best friends but she went because she loved Naomi a lot.

In the story of the Lost Sheep the boy felt frightened because he thought the sheep was going to die. When he found the sheep he was very glad because he loved the sheep.

When Moses was born the king was going to kill every boy in the country. Moses's mum hid him in the bulrushes because she loved her child.

Summary

Leader: Paul said that there are three things that will last forever – faith, hope and love. But of these, the greatest is love.

Love is the central message of the Bible. Christians believe that God sent his Son to live on the earth because he loved the world. If there is one word which sums up God, it is the word 'love'.

The Bible says 'God is love' and those who live in love, live in God and God lives in them.

Prayer

Dear God
Let love abide here in our school
Love of one another
Love of mankind
Love of life itself

Song: 'Come, Lord Jesus, come' (BBP 29)
(*the song is interspersed with the prayers*)

Dear God, please bless all those whom we love and those who love us.

Song: 'Come, Lord Jesus, come' (as above)

Dear God, let us remember that as many hands build a house, so many hearts make a school. Help us to live in love by showing our love in what we say and do.

Song: 'Come, Lord Jesus, come' (as above)

Leader: Love is a skill which everyone can develop – Christians believe it just needs a loving heart.

Song: 'Love will never come to an end' (C & P 99)

8.2 FEELINGS (REMEMBRANCE)

The starting point here is Remembrance Day, based on a lesson on the evacuation of children away from the bombing raids in the cities to the safety of the countryside. The written work includes children's feelings during a bombing raid, their feelings on leaving home and being in the country with strangers, and reflective prayers based on a compilation of 'I like it' statements about living in the country.

Song: 'Peace is flowing like a river' (C & P 144)

Introduction

Explain the background to how this work came to be written.

Dramatic readings of children's written work, interspersed with sound effects: 'Bombing raid in London' ('Spectacular Sound Effects', EMI, CDP 7951432).

Describe a group of children alone in their own house when an air raid starts, followed by

the sound of bombing. How did the children feel: lonely, scared, worried about parents?

Poems

Children's poems to reflect these feelings, read by children:

The bombing from the sky

Now the sirens started
Nothing stops the bombs whizzing
    through the sky
Blasting houses and rocks
Flying downwards
Crashing and crackling as they fall
Pounding in your ears
Blasting in your eyes.
Now the bombing's ended
Step outside.

Frightened in the shelter

Thirsty, hungry, scared.
Soggy, wet, damp and feeling ill.
Mucky, droopy, squashed and tired.
Terrified, petrified and horrified.
Dirty, sticky, scruffy.
That's me.
All over, all over.
Saved again!

In the Anderson shelter

I feel wet and I just met a little mouse.
He must feel uncomfortable like me.
Oh mouse, do you wish the war was
    ended?
Little mouse, I'm so cold, are you?
I wish I could see Mum and Dad.
Do you hear the all clear?
Yes, it's over!

Letters

Explain about evacuees being taken to the country for safety. Saying goodbye and then being collected by strangers when they reach the country. How did the children feel?

'Dear Mum' letters reflecting both feelings of sadness as well as relief to be away from the harsh reality of war, read by children:

Dear Mummy, I live on a farm in the country now. It is very quiet in the country. I wake up in the morning and help to milk the cows. I get the eggs. We have to look in the hay and in boxes and we have to have a basket to put the eggs in very carefully. I go to the shop to buy ham for breakfast. Auntie Sue is very nice. I like her and she likes me. I have made some new friends on the farm. My friends' names are Hannah and Jo and Jenny and they all live on the farm with me. I am a good cook now because I help to make breakfast and lunch and tea every day. Are you all right mum? I hope you are not hurt or frightened by the bombing. I am missing you a lot. Love from Anita XXX

Dear Mum, it is different here in the village shop. The food is very different. For breakfast I had fried egg, sausage and bacon. I have to collect the eggs from the chickens everyday. I have found that eggs don't just come in powder. They come in oval shapes and wiggly shapes and lump shapes too. I paddle in the stream behind our house and I get books from the shop. I have got twelve books so far. Love from Richard.

Dear Mum, I am on a farm with Mrs Hobbs. I am eating sausages and eggs and bacon. I have seen a cow. They are black and white. The cows go 'moo'. They give you milk. I'm two inches higher than last year. I am missing you mum. Is dad still fighting in France? Have you had a letter from dad yet mum? I like Mrs Hobbs, mum, because she doesn't let me go hungry. Love from Luke XXXXXXXXX

Prayer

Prayers, read by children, using a selection of children's thoughts about living in the country, away from the bombing, each beginning 'I like it because . . .'

I like it because I can paddle in the stream.
I like it because there are no bombs.
I like it because you can make good friends.
I like it because the food is better.
I like it because we can play hide and seek in the barns and fields.
I like it because I can run across the fields.
I like it because it is peaceful and quiet.
I like it because I can climb lots of trees.
I like it because there are lots of friendly people here.
I like it because it is safer.
I like it because I can play football.
I like it because I can have lots of picnics.
I like it because I can have a lot more food.
I like it because the house is warm and cosy.
I like it because you can pick the colourful flowers.
I like it because the school is kind to me.
I like it because I can have a vegetable patch.
I like it because I can feed the animals.
I like it because I can feed the birds.
I like it because I have eggs to eat.
I want to bring my mum and live here.

Song: 'Down by the riverside' (C & P 142)

Going-out music: 'We'll meet again' (Glen Miller Big Band Music)

8.3 SPECIAL PLACES

This act of worship was inspired by a visit to Whitby Abbey. The object is to reflect together on special places and how they have a kind of timelessness; and in a time of rapid change, to think about the things that endure.

Resources   Slides of school visit to Whitby Abbey.

Introductory music: 'Strange how my heart' (Enya, from *Shepherd's Moon*, WEA Records).

Introduction

Remind the children of the visit to Whitby. Show selected slides: the abbey; fossils on the beach; St Mary's; Caedmon's cross.

Writings

Children's written work (read out by the children). The examples here are by Year Five and Year Six children.

The Ammonite

A sparkling whorl
Encrusted spiral of creature long
    dead.
Eighty million years of waiting.
While eons roll into ages
While time slips past
It waits.
Until one day
Some schoolboy with his hammer
Seeking for fossils
As taught by his teacher
Unearths you and shows
You his world.
He holds in his hands
A fragile fragment of history
God's masterpiece
Resting in his open hands.

(Michael Pearson)

The Abbey

When I got to the Abbey I was surprised; it has a peaceful feeling in it. I feel like I can hear whispers sailing on the wind, it is silent like being in harmony with the world. It's a sad but happy feeling. Strong and beautiful land. Lands stretch for miles and miles. Cries and joy still stuck in the Abbey's walls. Walls still strong and stiff and others give way, peace and silence still strong. Not much change, throughout the land is peace, eternal peace. The Lord still looking down on these creations of his. History lies throughout these cold stone walls. The Abbey's future not yet decided. Will it crumble into pebbles or stay strong for generations to come?

(Ryan Goodwin)

Reflection

The leader takes the children through a 'quietening' procedure, for example: Hands and bodies still, relaxed; eyes closed; mind quiet. Think of yourselves in a 'bubble' of quiet stillness, separate from everyone else. Quietness and peace.

Remind the children that Jesus said he was like a vine – a provider of nourishment to all the branches; we are the branches.

Song: 'You are the Vine' (MP 792)

Prayer

'God be in my head' (use the words of the song, SoP 501)

Going-out music: 'Strange how my heart' (Enya).

9 Celebrating different faiths

There is, of course, a difference between religious education and collective worship. Religious education nowadays is a study of Christianity and other faiths, to develop knowledge and understanding, together with asking fundamental questions about life and death and trying to come to decisions about one's own faith and belief. Collective worship assumes some kind of consensus of shared belief, which is celebrated through prayer and praise; in county schools it has to be 'wholly or mainly of a broadly Christian character', and in church schools has to be 'in accordance with the school's Trust Deed' (this is usually taken to mean 'in accordance with the beliefs and practice of the church').

Despite these restrictions on collective worship, it is possible, with care and sensitivity, for aspects of faiths other than Christian to be celebrated in worship, whatever the racial and faith mix of the school. The starting point should not be pretence – we are not 'pretending' to be Jews in order to celebrate Pesach, or to be Sikhs in order to celebrate Guru Nanak's birthday; nor should the starting point be syncretism, which ignores differences and implies that all religions are equal and the same. The approach should be educational; this is, after all, collective worship in school we are talking about! Clearly the religious calendar could be one starting point: 'Today is the day when members of the _____ faith celebrate the birthday of their founder _____', for example. Another way would be to retell the story, historical or mythical, which lies behind a particular festi-

val. A third approach would be to tell a story from another tradition, just as a good story, with or without a religious or moral point.

Note: The question often arises: Do you use prayers from other traditions in collective worship? I'm inclined to say, 'Why not?'. After all, we regularly use Christian prayers, and this is an unfamiliar religion to many children. The only caveat I would suggest is that we should be careful how we introduce prayers. A form of words which might be suitable is along these lines:

> I am going to read a prayer which comes from the —— tradition, and which would be said during the festival we have just been hearing about. Please close your eyes and think hard about what this prayer would mean for the followers of the —— faith, and what it might mean for you.

This takes a lot longer to say than 'Let us pray', but it is more intellectually honest and more appropriate to the school setting.

9.1 DIWALI

Beginning with a description of how Hindus celebrate Diwali, this act of worship goes on to retell in a dramatic way the story of Rama and Sita, which is the basis of the festival of Diwali. Is it worship? In so far as it is a celebration of an important element of the religious education curriculum, yes; and in so far as it is an insight through story into deep, powerful emotions of loyalty, love and good triumphing over evil, again yes.

Type of worship Whole class for the school.

Setting School hall with decorated backdrop of Diwali work.

Resources Divas, matches, costumes/puppet theatre and puppets/bow, sari, duster, garland, diwali cards and sweets (made by children), Rangoli patterns (made by children), lentils, beans, pulses, coloured sand and templates, face paints, Mendhi patterns (designed by children), paintings of goddess Lakshmi, incense sticks, instruments, Indian music.

Child: Diwali is a Hindu festival of lights.

Child: Diwali means row of lights.

Teacher: We have made divas to hold candles just like Hindus who celebrate Diwali.

Children show their divas and tell everyone how they made them.

Teacher: Diwali is also about good winning over evil so the story of Rama and Sita is told. We will hear the story in a moment. But first, we have been finding out what people do at Diwali time.

Child: They buy new clothes (*show sari*).

Child: They clean the house (*pretend to dust*).

Child: They decorate the house (*show garland*).

Child: They give cards (*give out handmade Diwali cards*).

Child: They make special sweets (*give out*).

Teacher: At Diwali time people put special patterns on their hands (*show drawings of patterns*).

Child: Real patterns are made with henna.

Child: They are called Mendhi patterns (*show painted hands – use face paints*).

Teacher: They also make another type of pattern called Rangoli patterns; we have made some with rice, lentils and beans (*show patterns*); we have also made a large Rangoli pattern with sand and powder paint (*show this*). Rangoli patterns were made to show lotuses for the goddess Lakshmi (*show pictures drawn of her*). She is the goddess of wealth. At Diwali time people light divas to welcome her good luck into their homes and to remember the story of Rama and Sita.

Light divas and incense. Sing Diwali song with actions. Play instruments, maracas, Indian bells and shakers.

Story/Play

Narrator: There was once a princess called Sita. She had a special bow. She would only marry the prince who could string her bow. Many princes came to try their luck but none could string the bow.

At this time there was a King who had three Queens who all had sons. One son was called Rama and he was kind and gentle. He decided to try his luck with the bow. Skilfully he took the bow and began to string it.

Rama: I've strung the bow.

Narrator: So Rama and Sita were married (*play music*). They then went home to see Rama's father the King and Rama's mother the Queen. The King said:

King: You can be king now, Rama.

Narrator: The Queen was jealous because she wanted Rama's brother Bharata to be king. She said to the King:

Queen: Send Rama and Sita away for 14 years.

Narrator: The King had to agree. So Rama and Sita went to live in the forest. When Bharata heard what his mother had done he said:

Bharata: I will not be king. I think Rama should be king.

Narrator: Rama had another brother, Lakshmana, who loved him very much. When Lakshmana heard what Bharata had said, he decided he must tell Rama. He said:

Lakshmana: I will go and look for Rama and Sita.

Narrator: So off he went into the forest.

Deep in the forest a wicked demoness Surpanaka watched Rama. While Sita was away she went to see Rama.

Surpanaka: Rama, I love you, come with me.

Rama: No, for it is Sita I love.

Narrator: Lakshmana heard voices and came out of the hut and scared Surpanaka away. Surpanaka went to find her brother, Ravana, the ten-headed demon.

Surpanaka: Help me to get Rama and you can have Sita.

Narrator: So they hatched a plan. Ravana came and tricked Sita.

Ravana: Come with me, Sita.

Narrator: Then he showed her who he was.

Sita: Help!

Narrator: Rama realized that Sita had gone and he felt very sad. Lakshmana found Rama wandering in the forest.

Rama: Lakshmana, Ravana has taken Sita away.

Lakshmana: Let's get help.

Narrator: They found Hanuman the monkey king.

Hanuman: I will help you to find Sita.

Narrator: Eventually, they found Ravana and Sita. Rama and his good friends fought Ravana and his evil army (*shaking tambourine*). Eventually Rama won.

All: Hurray.

Sita: Thank you, Rama.

Narrator: Rama and Sita went home and Rama became the King. Everyone lit lamps and decorated their homes to welcome home Rama and Sita.

End by playing Indian music and giving the children a short opportunity for reflection.

9.2 FRIENDSHIP

A celebration of friendship in two religions, Christianity and Hinduism.

No attempt to compare or contrast, just to draw out good things from each.

Resources Large cards with letters J,O,Y; large pictures, painted by children, depicting incidents from the Gospels; Rahki bracelets.

Introductory song: 'With a little help from my friends' (A 38)

Introduction

The leader, or one of the children, explains what this act of worship is about.

Narrator 1: Christians believe they have real JOY when they (J) – put Jesus first, (O) – put others next, (Y) – put

yourself last. (*Children hold the cards up at the appropriate point*)

Narrator 2: In the Bible there are many stories of people thinking of others. (*Painted pictures held up with labels*)

- The little boy who gave up his own lunch to share.

- Friends of the paralysed man who took him to see Jesus.

- The Samaritan who stopped to help the man lying in the road.

- Jesus who died on a cross – for us.

Narrator 3: We should try to think of others. Hindu girls remember their brothers every year at a special festival. They give their brothers a Rahki bracelet and cards are given out to say 'Thank you, Brother, for looking after me and being so special.' (*Girls give bracelets and tie on to their brothers' wrists at this point. Or, if no Hindu artefacts are available, make friendship braided bracelets with thick wool*)

Narrator 1: Even special friends are given bracelets. (*Again, tie on to friends' wrists*)

Narrator 2: Brothers promise once again to look after their sisters and be special friends to them. They do this even when they grow up and get married.

Narrator 3: We can be friends with our brothers and sisters and each other. Here is a poem to remind us just how special friends are.

Poem: 'Friends' (*Read by a group of children*)

(from Margaret Cooling, *Assemblies for Primary Schools*, RMEP, 1990)

Song: 'Magic penny' ('Love is something if you give it away') (A 10)

Leader: Now let's sit quietly and think about our own friends and brothers and sisters – or you can pray quietly with us.

Children stand and recite own prepared thoughts/prayers about friends, etc.

Concluding music: Adult plays 'Magic penny' on piano as school leads out.

9.3 PASSOVER

This is a simple way of celebrating the Jewish festival of Pesach, Passover, based around a retelling of the event on which the festival is based. This is quite long, and could be spread over several days.

Resources Seder dish, parsley in salt water; unleavened bread; a roasted egg; shank bone of lamb; haroset (a mixture of apples, nuts, cinnamon and wine).

Introductory music: 'When Israel was in Egypt's land' ('Let my people go')

Leader: Pesach (Passover) is the Jewish festival which celebrates the exodus from Egypt of the Israelites. The name Passover comes from the biblical story of the plague in which the first-born of every Egyptian household was killed, but the angel of God passed over the Israelite houses and their first-born were not killed.

The following account is a simplified retelling of Exodus chapters 5–15. It lends itself to being read by five voices: the Narrator, Moses, Pharaoh, Yahweh, and a messenger.

Narrator: The Israelites were slaves in Egypt. Moses had been told by Yahweh – the Israelite name for God – to go back to Egypt and persuade Pharaoh, the Egyptian king, to let the Israelites go. He went back and was met by his brother Aaron.

Because of his upbringing, Moses could always get to see Pharaoh, and he and Aaron went to the court at once.

Moses: My Lord Pharaoh. We represent the leaders of your servants, the Israelites. We seek permission to leave the country for a few days to worship our god Yahweh in the wilderness, as he has commanded.

Pharaoh: Yahweh? Who is he? Never heard of him. Not one of our gods.

Narrator: Pharaoh consulted with his advisors, then turned back to Moses and Aaron.

Pharaoh: Request denied. Get back to work at once, all of you.

Narrator: Moses and Aaron, who had been warned by God that it would not be easy to convince Pharaoh, were not surprised by his hardness, and left quietly.

Pharaoh: They're trouble-makers. The Israelites always were an idle lot. Keep them hard at work, flog a few of them as an example, and cut off their straw ration. Tell them we still want the same number of bricks, but they'll have to find their own straw.

Narrator: The Israelites, already grumbling about the amount of work they had to do, now had to scavenge for stubble and straw every morning to make the number of bricks the Egyptians demanded. Moses and Aaron were very unpopular, and when the floggings began, Moses decided it was time for another visit to Pharaoh. At the court, Moses repeated his request to let the Israelites go, and as he expected, Pharaoh again refused.

Moses: I will show you the power of our God, Yahweh.

Narrator: Moses threw his staff on the floor, and as in the desert, it turned into a snake. Pharaoh was startled at this, but his chief magician came and whispered in his ear, and he turned back to Moses with a smile.

Pharaoh: Cheap tricks! You won't catch me like that. My magicians can do that sort of thing – they do it all the time.

Narrator: Next morning, Moses and Aaron met Pharaoh on the banks of the Nile as he was going to worship the river-god.

Moses: Pharaoh... will you let us go?

Narrator: Again Pharaoh refused.

Moses: Then watch.

Narrator: He turned, and struck the waters of the Nile with his staff. At once the waters turned to blood, and the fish started to die. Again, Pharaoh's magicians claimed they could do the same, and Pharaoh would not give way. The Egyptians had to dig new wells for drinking water, and the plague lasted for seven days. Moses again prayed to Yahweh, and returned to Pharaoh again.

Moses: Unless you let us go, Yahweh will send a plague of frogs which will swarm all over the land. They will be in your houses, in your cooking pots, in your beds, everywhere.

Narrator: Pharaoh shuddered, but still would not change his mind. Moses stretched out his hand, and the frogs began to appear, just as he had said. Pharaoh's magicians were powerless to drive them away, and Pharaoh called Moses and Aaron back to him.

Pharaoh: Ask your god to take the frogs away. When they've gone, I'll let the Israelites go.

Narrator: Moses agreed, and told Pharaoh the frogs would be gone by the next day. But as soon as the frogs were gone, Pharaoh changed his mind again, and refused to let the Israelites go. This went on for months. Moses threatened plagues of gnats, plagues of flies, a pestilence on the cattle, an outbreak of boils, hailstorms, a plague of locusts, even the threat of darkness over the whole land. Nothing would change Pharaoh's mind. He would refuse to listen to Moses, Moses would tell Yahweh, the plague would come about, and Pharaoh would agree to let the people go. Then, as soon as the plague was lifted, Pharaoh would change his mind again. It seemed to Moses as if Yahweh was toying with Pharaoh – teasing him and tormenting him, but not dealing the final blow which would convince him.

Yahweh: All right, Moses, I have one more plague for the Egyptians. This will be the last straw for Pharaoh, and he will let you go this time. Tell the people of Israel to slaughter a lamb or a kid, one for every household. They are to smear the doorposts of their houses with the animals' blood, then roast the meat. I shall kill the first-born child of every family in Egypt, but I will see the blood on the Israelite doorposts and pass over those houses.

Narrator: Moses and Aaron gave Yahweh's instructions to the Israelites, and before midnight that night, the Lord struck just as he had said. Pharaoh, torn with grief and anger, called Moses and Aaron to him in the middle of the night, and ordered the Israelites to leave at once. They took their belongings, their cattle and sheep, and set off towards Succoth, a long train of men and women, children and animals. They left so suddenly that they didn't even have time to leaven the bread they had been baking. Moses led the way, following the sign Yahweh had given him: a pillar of cloud by day, and a pillar of fire by night. They came to the Sea of Reeds, a swampy, dangerous area, and Moses ordered them to camp for the night. Meanwhile, Pharaoh was having second thoughts yet again. All that slave labour; was he wise to let them go? Just then, a messenger from the Etham garrison, near the Sea of Reeds, burst in.

Messenger: My Lord! The Israelites are escaping! They are at Etham, and trying to cross the Sea of Reeds!

Narrator: Furious, Pharaoh ordered his chariots to set off in pursuit and bring the Israelites back. When the Israelites heard Pharaoh's army catching up with them, and saw they were cut off by the swamp, they turned on Moses and Aaron.

All readers: Were there no graves in Egypt, that you had to bring us to die here in the wilderness?

Yahweh: Tell them not to panic. Stretch out your staff over the waters, and a path will open up for you. Tell the people to strike camp and follow you across. I will deal with the Egyptians.

Narrator: Moses did as Yahweh commanded, and the Israelites crossed safely through the swamp to dry land. As they watched, the Egyptians' chariots thundered into the swamp and became bogged down. Hampered by their heavy armour, the Egyptian soldiers floundered in the waters and many of them were drowned. Yahweh had saved Israel, and the people once

again put their trust in Yahweh and Moses.

Leader: So why do you think the festival is called Passover? (*Draw out from the children that Yahweh, or his angel, 'passed over' the Israelite houses*)

On Passover Eve, the men go to the synagogue, then return home for a special meal, the Seder. Seder means order, and there is a special order of service, written in a book called the Haggadah (telling), which tells the story of Passover. The meal starts with the blessing of the wine; four glasses of wine are drunk during the meal, as a reminder of God's four promises to Moses (Exodus chapter 6, verses 6, 7).

The meal itself has a number of symbolic items: parsley in salt water (the bitterness of slavery); three pieces of unleavened bread, or matzoth (the hurried departure, when the Israelites had no time to leaven the dough); a baked or roasted egg (representing the hope of new life); a roasted shank bone of lamb (the lamb which was sacrificed); and a mixture of apples, nuts, cinnamon and wine, called haroset (the mortar used by the Hebrew slaves in Egypt).

The youngest boy asks 'Why is this night different from all other nights?' The child then asks four questions about the Passover, the answers to which tell the story of the night when the Israelites escaped from Egypt. A fifth cup of wine is traditionally left untouched for the prophet Elijah, whose return would mean the coming of the Messiah.

Children may be allowed to taste the parsley in salt water, the matzoth, and the haroset.

Song: 'What about being old Moses?' (C & P 81)

Reflective prayer

We remember the time when the Israelites were suffering as slaves in Egypt, and we think of people all over the world today who are suffering under cruel and oppressive governments. We pray that they may be given hope and new lives as the Israelites were.

We thank God for the courage of Moses in standing up to Pharaoh, and we pray that we too may be brave if we come across injustice or cruelty.

9.4 GURU GOBIND RAI AND THE FORMATION OF THE KHALSA

The spring harvest festival in India, Baisakhi, has become for Sikhs a commemoration of the formation of the Khalsa – the brotherhood of Sikhs. This act of worship re-enacts the events of Baisakhi 1699, and provides a stimulus to follow-up work in the classroom, along the lines of 'What do you think happened?'

Setting Curtains, which can be drawn across to symbolize the tent. Drama block for the dais.

Resources Large (wooden or cardboard!) sword. Costumes for Guru Gobind Rai and the five Sikh volunteers – simple loincloth at first, 'uniforms' for the ending – or just turbans. Cooking pot.

Introduction

The extent to which this introduction is necessary will depend upon whether the subject has been covered in RE.

Leader: In the sixteenth century of the Common Era, northern India was overrun by the Moghuls. They converted millions to their faith, Islam, at the point of the sword. The leaders of the Sikh religion, the Gurus, always stood up for the freedom of the individual, and many of them were martyred (that is, killed for their beliefs). One of the Gurus, Guru Gobind Rai, decided that the time had come for Sikhs to stand up and fight for their beliefs. The story that follows dates from 1699. No one can say precisely what took place, but many Sikhs believe that it happened exactly as recounted here.

Story

The version of the story which follows lends itself to a dramatic reading involving seven people: a narrator, Guru Gobind Rai, Daya Ram, Dharam Das, Mokham Chand, Sahib Chand, and Himmat Rai. A minimum of rehearsal is required: all the five 'volunteers' have to do is get up at the appropriate point and go behind the curtain, then appear suitably dressed at the end.

Narrator: Gobind Rai thought for a long time about the crisis that was facing his followers. He was opposed to the political tyranny of the Moghuls, but he was also opposed to the old social and religious tyranny of the rigid Hindu caste system, in which the priestly caste lorded it over all others. On the occasion of the Baisakhi celebrations, the April harvest festival of the year 1699, Gobind Rai called together Sikhs from all over India to the Punjab. Eighty thousand Sikhs responded to the Guru's call. A large tent was pitched in front of the assembly, and when everyone had arrived and sat down, Guru Gobind Rai emerged from the tent and stood on a dais in front of the gathering with a drawn sword.

Gobind Rai: My faithful Sikhs. Is there anyone here who would lay down his life for his beliefs? I want the head of a Sikh. I must have a sacrifice.

Narrator: And he brandished the sword above his head fiercely. There was a murmur of astonishment among the assembled ranks, but no response. The Guru repeated his challenge, and again no one moved. At the third call, a man called Daya Ram stepped forward and bowed to the Guru.

Daya Ram: My Lord. My head is yours, to dispose of as you will.

Narrator: Gobind Rai led him into the tent. The assembled Sikhs rose to their feet expectantly. There was a swish, a thud, and those nearest the tent saw a stream of blood coming from under the canvas. The Guru emerged with his great sword dripping fresh blood. He held it aloft, and the people shrank back.

Gobind Rai: I want another head! My sword wants to taste the blood of another beloved Sikh. We must sacrifice to gain our freedom.

Narrator: At this, there was much muttering and stirring among the people, and many began to slink away. But one stood up and came forward – Dharam Das, of Delhi. He too offered his head to the Guru, and was led into the tent. Again came the swish and thud, and once more blood flowed.

The Guru came out again with the same demand, and one after another three more Sikhs came forward – Mokham Chand, Sahib Chand and Himmat Rai. One by one they faced the ordeal of the dripping sword. Five brave Sikhs had faced the Guru's supreme test.

Then a remarkable thing happened. Before the eyes of the astonished assembly, the Guru came out of the tent – accompanied by the same five Sikhs! They were wearing new uniforms, and glowing with new confidence.

The five emerge, with Guru Gobind Rai. They place the iron pot on the dais and sit round it. Gobind Rai stirs it with a two-edged sword.

Narrator: The Guru, helped by his five 'beloved ones', prepared an iron pot of 'amrit', a nectar made from sugar cakes and water, stirred with a khanda or double-edged sword. Gobind Rai then gave some of the amrit to each of his five disciples; in this way he declared them all equal, and so abolished the hated caste system.

The five were given a new surname, Singh, added to their names. The Guru himself received the amrit from the five, and took the name Guru Gobind Singh. Singh means 'brave as a lion'. Soon the Guru had an army of followers, all prepared to die for their faith; all had taken the amrit and assumed the surname Singh. This army became known as the order of the Khalsa – the army of soldier saints.

Song: 'He who would valiant be' (C & P 44) or 'When a knight won his spurs' (C & P 50)

Prayer

Thank you, Lord, for religious leaders of all faiths, to whom you have spoken down the centuries. Today we remember Guru Gobind Rai and the challenge he put to his people. Thank you for the courage of those first five soldier saints of Sikhism, and for all who have had the courage to stand up for what they believe – even to the point of death. Help us to have the courage to stand up for what we believe, and not to be put off even if people laugh at us or mock us. Amen.

10 Writing and telling stories

The most common form of collective worship in schools is where the leader of worship reads a story from one of the hundreds of collections of stories put together for this purpose. Nothing wrong with that! Many of those collections are full of good, interesting, enjoyable stories, which make strong moral, religious or spiritual points, and are worth telling again and again.

The purpose of this chapter, however, is not simply to add to the collection of 'assembly stories' to be used in this way, although it does contain six stories which form the core of six acts of worship. Rather, the intention is to encourage you, the reader and leader of collective worship, to write your own stories,

in your own words, by giving you some examples which have been written by teachers and leaders of collective worship in schools.

Sometimes you can think of quite an original story. Not everyone can do this, but if you can, then just write it down and tell it. It may have a strong, implicit 'moral'; the story of 'The Christmas Pudding', for example, draws a parallel between the ingredients of the pudding, and the make up of the human race and what binds us together. Other stories may be simply stories, but lend themselves to collective worship just because they are about people and feelings and relationships.

Animal stories have been a powerful source of invention from Aesop onwards. The story of the two frogs could be used as a moral to keep on trying, but here it is used as an example of friendship. Sometimes these examples don't bear too close an analysis; what sort of friend is it who encourages you to jump into a churn of milk and get stuck? What would the farmer think? But as a story for Key Stage 1 children, this could be fun to tell and a simple moral tale. 'The earthquake', another animal story, is based on the Pali Jatakas, Buddhist birth stories which relate the supposed former existences of the Buddha. Myths and legends from the world's religions are a splendid starting point for the would-be storyteller, because all you have to do is take the story and retell it in your own words – as here.

Stories of the saints, from the Christian tradition, also abound, but need retelling both to make them accessible to today's children, and to bring out the points we want to emphasize – in the case of St Francis, his love for (and power over) animals as God's creatures, and in the case of St Hugh of Lincoln, his 'common touch' and love for ordinary people.

Another good source of stories for the would-be storyteller is the history of the Christian Church. Take an incident such as the story of the Pilgrim Fathers, look it up in a history book in the library, then recount it, or an aspect of it, in your own words, emphasizing the point you want to celebrate in worship – in this case, the courage of the Pilgrim Fathers and their determination to worship God in what they felt to be the right way.

10.1 THE CHRISTMAS PUDDING

Theme The ingredients of the Christmas pudding are seen to symbolize all the different people in the world.

Setting The children sit on the floor, lights are low, candles lit.

Resources Christmas pudding ingredients ready to hand, with large spoon and bowl.

Introductory music: Any soft 'Christmas' theme music.

Leader: Welcome the children.

Story

The Christmas pudding (*This could be read by two voices: father and child*)

The minute I opened my eyes, I knew something was different. As I peeped out from under my quilt my bedroom looked different. What was it? What was different this morning? It was a little bit colder in my bedroom than usual. Everything seemed hushed and still. Soft white light filtered through my curtains. I pushed back the quilt, stepped out of bed and went to the window. Throwing back the curtains I saw it. Snow had fallen in the night while I was asleep. My garden was transformed into a white winter wonderland. I gazed in wonder at the velvety white snow. It had covered the grass, like a white fur coat and it had sprinkled the trees with icing sugar.

'Come on! Stir yourself, there's a Christmas pudding to be made today.'

My dad was shouting to me from the kitchen. I hurried into my clothes, shivering as I dressed. I said good morning to my woolly teddy bear and kissed him on the nose, before rushing downstairs. The kitchen was warm and cosy. Two of our cats lay purring,

sleepy and full of milk, next to the Aga. There was a delicious smell of butter and spices.

'Come on, little mix-up,' said my dad. He had a lovely warm smile on his face and I noticed he had flour on his nose.

'Eat your porridge,' said Dad, 'and you can put syrup in it for a special treat. Oh! And go to the back door and call Smuffles. The other two cats have had their breakfast, but I haven't seen Smuffles yet this morning.'

I opened the kitchen door and looked outside. Snow covered the doorstep. Carefully I put my toe into the crisp dry snow and leaned out further into the garden.

'Smuffles . . . Smuffles!' I called. Smuffles heard my call and peeped out from behind the plant pot. 'Miaow!' He didn't like the feel of the cold snow on his paws. 'Smuffles, you silly cat,' I giggled. 'Come on . . . be brave, it's nice and warm in the kitchen.'

With all three cats safely inside snoozing and dreaming, it was time to make our Christmas pudding.

'Raisins first,' said Dad. 'Put them in the bowl. Currants and sultanas next.' I dipped my fingers into the bowl of dried fruit.

'What are raisins and currants and sultanas, Dad? Do they grow on trees?' Dad laughed. 'Grapes,' he said, 'different kinds of grapes, picked from the vine in the hot countries where they grow and spread out in the sun to dry.'

'But how can they all be grapes?' I said. 'They all look different. Currants are little and hard. Raisins are just raisins, and sultanas are soft and gooey.'

'It's like people,' said Dad. 'We're all the same really, but we look different and we have different characters. It wouldn't do for us all to be the same, would it?'

'Breadcrumbs next,' he said, and handed me a wooden spoon. I poured the soft white breadcrumbs on top of the raisins and currants and sultanas, covering them like snow. I mixed them all up together. Then I tasted some of the mixture. The fruit was delicious, but the breadcrumbs were – just breadcrumbs.

'Why do we put breadcrumbs in?' I said. Dad laughed. 'Here, stir the flour in too. Breadcrumbs and flour make the pudding strong. The pudding would collapse without them!'

'Like you!' I said. 'You're strong, Dad!'

'Now for the sugar,' he said.

'Yum, yum, I love sugar,' I said, tasting a bit on my finger. 'Sugar is sweet and delicious and nice and . . .

'Who do you know who's sweet?' said Dad.

I thought for a minute. 'My teddy!'

Dad laughed again. He put more things in the mixture – suet, to make the pudding moist, eggs to make the pudding rich and fluffy. 'Now for the spices,' he said. 'Nutmeg and cinnamon, to add a Christmassy flavour. Give it a good stir now!'

I pushed the spoon round the mixture and thought about the pudding. It was funny to think that all those different ingredients, mixed up together, could make one round fat Christmas pudding.

It's like the world, I thought – a big round ball, made of different countries and people.

'Come on little pudding-face,' my dad said, shaking me out of my daydream, 'make a wish!'

We both held the wooden spoon and stirred. I closed my eyes and wished. For the best Christmas ever.

Discussion

The children are shown the Christmas pudding ingredients, one by one, and each one is discussed as in the story, e.g.:

- Fruit = different characters of people who make up the world – we are all different.

- Sugar = the nice things in our lives, treats, special events.

- Breadcrumbs/flour = strength and security of our parents and helpers.

Then mix all the ingredients together and make the pudding, ready for cooking.

Song: 'Bind us together Lord' (MP 54)

Prayer

Dear Jesus, we are all different, and we are all part of your world. We know that you love us all equally. Help us to love one another and to care for each other day by day. Thank you for our parents and helpers, who love us and give us strength and room to grow. We thank you, Jesus, for all the good things in our lives – special treats and presents. And thank you, too, for Christmas pudding! Amen.

Going-out music: 'We wish you a Merry Christmas'.

If possible, cook the pudding later and allow the children to see it and sample it.

10.2 FRIENDSHIP

Age range: Key Stage 1

Theme Helping one another

Introductory music: Pachelbel, Canon in D Minor.

Introduction

Question: Why do we need friends? Who can be our friend? (adults, pets, etc.)

Activity: Invite a child out to fold a travel rug/small sheet neatly. When the child has difficulty, ask for suggestions as to how to overcome the problem. Invite a friend to help. With two, the task is easier.

Story

One hot summer's day two frogs were hopping down the lane. They came to a farmyard. 'Oh look,' said the big frog, 'a farmyard. We will be able to go and get a cool, refreshing drink of milk to quench our thirst – and it will make us big and strong!'

'Oh no!' said the little frog, 'I can't go across the farmyard, I will get trampled on. Just look at all those great big animals with their great big feet.' Moo,' said the cow. 'Neigh,' said the horse. 'Oh come on!' said the big frog, boasting. 'I can get across easily – just follow me!'

'Oh dear, please don't go!' said the little frog, but the big frog was already halfway across the farmyard and the little frog shouted, 'Wait for me, please don't leave me – I can't do this journey alone.'

Big frog stopped, turned around and went back for his friend little frog. Big frog said, 'Stay close and I will help you.' Together they set off across the farmyard. 'Quack,' said the duck. 'Woof,' said the sheepdog. The frogs hopped from stone to stone until they reached the shiny milk churn. 'Follow me,' said big frog and with a mighty leap he landed with a plop in the beautiful, cool, creamy milk.

'Come on in, it's gorgeous – there's lots to drink,' shouted big frog.

'Alright,' said little frog, 'here I come.' One, two, three . . . And in plopped little frog. Oh what fun they had splashing and swimming and drinking.

'I've had enough now,' said big frog. 'Let's get out and head for home.' But . . . the top of the churn was too high. The level of milk had gone down while they had been drinking. They just couldn't jump out. Although they tried and tried it was no use. 'Oh no,' said big frog with a weary, sad voice, 'I can't go on trying, I'm too tired.'

'Oh yes you can – don't give up now, big frog – keep on paddling – I'm sure help will come soon.'

'I'm sinking,' said big frog.

'Hold my front leg,' said little frog, 'I'll help you – just like you helped me across the farmyard.'

Together they kept on paddling until the creamy milk turned to butter and they were

both able to jump from the butter out of the churn. 'Thank you,' said big frog.

'You're welcome,' said little frog, 'that's what friends are for.' And together they hopped back home.

Prayer

> Dear God, we know friends are special. Jesus was a special friend to lots of people long ago. Today he is still our friend. Help us to be a good friend to others. Amen.

Song: 'Cross over the road' (C & P 70)

Going-out music: Continuation of entering music.

10.3 THE EARTHQUAKE

This act of worship has been used in a number of different schools. The story originally comes from the Pali Jatakas (Buddhist birth stories) although, in different versions, the story is quite well known. Here it is retold in simple language for the primary school.

Theme Thinking for yourself.

Opening music: *The Carnival of the Animals* (Saint-Saëns).

Introduction

Explain that the point of this act of worship is to thank God for giving us brains to think for ourselves, not just to follow the herd.

The story of Sam the rabbit follows. Say that you are going to ask the children afterwards whether Sam had thought for himself.

Story

The story is presented here to be read by one voice, but could easily be modified so that the animals' lines are spoken by different children.

There was once a rabbit called Sam, who lived in a sandy bank under a large fruit tree, quite close to the sea and on the edge of a large forest. He was a rather nervous little rabbit and always had a good look round

before leaving the safety of his rabbit hole to go and search for food.

One day Sam was sitting under the fruit tree, twitching his nose and wiggling his whiskers and wondering what he would find for breakfast, when suddenly he had a thought. Now he wasn't a terribly intelligent rabbit and didn't often have thoughts, so this one rather took him by surprise. The thought that had struck him so suddenly was this: if the world should fall apart, what would happen to me? Now you have to admit, that is a rather frightening thought. The little rabbit imagined himself falling through space, his ears flapping and his paws waving, and it quite put him off his breakfast.

Anyway, after a while Sam put the thought out of his mind, and decided to set off in search of food. Just as he was having a look round the tree to make sure the coast was clear, an enormous ripe fruit fell out of the tree and landed cra-a-sh behind him. The rabbit shot three feet up in the air, convinced that his thought was coming true; the world was falling apart! Without stopping to look behind him, he laid back his ears and set off as fast as he could run.

Sam hadn't gone far when another rabbit saw him. 'What's up, Sam?' he asked urgently as Sam flashed past.

'The world is falling apart!' Sam shouted back without stopping.

The second rabbit didn't stop to think; he just laid back his ears and tore off after Sam through the forest. Before long there were twenty of them, then thirty, then forty, all rushing madly through the forest convinced that the world was falling apart. A wart-hog saw them and joined in, then a deer, then several more deer and three large giraffes, and finally a huge elephant. What had started off as Sam in a panic had now become a wild stampede crashing through the forest; all trying to get away because they thought the world was falling apart.

King Len heard the commotion and strolled out of his den to see what was going on. King Len was a magnificent lion with an enormous roar and a huge shaggy mane. When he saw the charging animals, led by the terrified Sam, he loped alongside them and asked what was happening.

'The world is falling apart! The world is falling apart! Run! Run for your life!' they gasped.

King Len was somewhat taken aback by this. 'I suppose they mean an earthquake,' he thought to himself. King Len was very well informed. 'They can't be right, or I would have heard it. Oh well. I'd better put a stop to all this before there's an accident.'

Taking a short cut he intercepted the column of running animals and roared his enormous roar. Sam stopped suddenly, and all the others piled up behind him. When they had sorted themselves out, King Len ambled down the line and asked them what the panic was all about.

'The world is falling apart! The world is falling apart!' they clamoured.

'Quiet!' ordered King Len. 'Now let's get this straight. Who has actually seen this happening? You, elephant?'

'Not me,' said the elephant. 'The giraffes saw it, and I followed them.'

'No we didn't,' admitted the giraffes. 'We followed the deer.'

'And we didn't actually see it – the wart-hog told us,' said the deer.

Finally the lion got to Sam. Sam felt very important. 'I saw it,' he announced proudly.

'I was sitting outside my rabbit hole, getting ready for breakfast, when it happened.'

'Oh yes?' said King Len innocently. 'What . . . ah . . . actually did happen?'

'Well – there was this terrific rumbling and crashing noise behind me, and so I ran,' said Sam.

'So – you didn't actually see what happened?' enquired King Len severely.

'Well – er – no – I suppose not,' admitted Sam. 'But I'm sure the world was falling apart.'

King Len sighed. 'We'd better go and have a look,' he said. 'Get on my back, Sam. Hold on to my mane. The rest of you wait here.'

Sam clambered up on to King Len's massive shoulders, and the lion loped off through the forest until he came to the sandbank where Sam lived.

'Is this where it happened?' he asked the rabbit.

'Y-y-yes, sir,' replied Sam, his teeth chattering with fear.

'Show me where you were sitting,' ordered King Len.

'J-j-j-just there, under that big tree, sir,' said Sam.

King Len had already seen that it was a fruit tree. 'Just as I thought,' he muttered to himself. He walked slowly over to the tree. Sam covered his face with his paws, fully expecting the lion to disappear into a large hole any minute.

'Come over here, Sam,' called out King Len.

'Oh n-n-no, sir, I d-d-daren't!' Sam cried, his ears laid back in terror.

'Sam,' said the king sternly.

Nervously, Sam opened his eyes and edged over to where he had been sitting when the earthquake occurred.

'There's your earthquake,' said King Len, pointing to the squashed remains of the large fruit which had fallen out of the tree.

'Oh – is – is that all?' asked Sam, now feeling rather foolish.

'That's all,' replied the lion. 'And now I think we'd better go and tell the others, don't you?'

'Er – yes, I suppose so,' said Sam, not looking forward to this at all.

When the other animals heard what had really happened, they began to laugh and jeer at poor Sam.

'Just a minute,' said King Len. 'Sam wasn't the only one to think it was an earthquake, was he? Was he, elephant? Was he, giraffes? Deer? Wart-hog?'

The other animals saw the point and slunk away, resolved not to be so silly in future. And Sam thanked King Len, and went off to have his breakfast at last.

So – did Sam think for himself?

Song: 'All creatures of our God and King' (C & P 7) or 'Song of Caedmon' (C & P 13) or 'Who put the colours in the rainbow?' (C & P 12)

Prayer

> Thank you, God, for giving us brains to think for ourselves. Help us to use our brains well, and to grow up to be sensible, thoughtful and helpful people. Help us not just to follow others, but to be brave enough to stand up for what we believe.

10.4 ST FRANCIS AND THE WOLF OF GUBBIO

Theme A holy man, who became a saint, whose faith in God was so great that he had an extraordinary, almost supernatural, power over animals.

Introductory music: Excerpt from *Peter and the Wolf.*

Story: Saint Francis and the Wolf of Gubbio

When Francis was very old, he would ride from place to place on a donkey with one of the brothers walking alongside. One cold winter, he was travelling in this way from the monastery at San Verecondo to the town of Gubbio, and walked quite safely through a forest despite warnings about the fierce wolves that were roaming freely there.

On arriving in Gubbio, Francis and the brother found the townspeople in a state of terror because of the wolves. It was so cold and the wolves were so hungry that they were virtually holding the town in a state of siege. One huge wolf in particular would come to the walls of the town quite openly and make off with animals and children.

Francis immediately said he would go and talk to the wolf. Everyone tried to dissuade him, but he insisted. A few friars went with him, and the townspeople followed as they approached the wolf's lair. When they were near the lair, Francis made the others stop and went on alone. The townspeople watched from a safe distance.

As Francis moved forward the wolf made ready to attack him, but Francis made a sign of the cross and cried out: 'Come here, Brother Wolf; in the name of Jesus Christ, you

are not to harm me or anyone else.' The effect was remarkable; it was as if the wolf recognized something more than human in Francis. He crawled to the man's feet and lay down. The danger was past.

'Now listen, Brother Wolf,' said Francis sternly. 'I know what you've been up to, but I know it was only because you were so hungry that you were so wicked.' Francis went on to suggest that if the wolf made peace with the inhabitants of Gubbio and promised not to harm their animals or children ever again, the townspeople on their part would provide him with food. The wolf seemed to understand, and bowed his head.

'If I arrange this for you,' Francis concluded, 'do you promise never again to attack another animal or human?' Francis held out his hand, and the wolf lifted up his paw and put it in Francis's hand, as if to say 'I promise'.

Then Francis told the wolf to follow him, and together they went back to Gubbio. The people parted to let them through, not knowing quite what to expect. When they reached the market place, Francis told the people about the understanding he had reached with the wolf, and made the wolf repeat his promise by placing his paw in Francis's hand in front of everyone.

People say that the wolf lived for two years in Gubbio, going from door to door for his food and always being very gentle and well-behaved. Then he died, and the people of Gubbio mourned his loss greatly.

It is of course easy to doubt the truth of this story, and some people have suggested that Brother Wolf was really a bandit whose fierce deeds had earned him the name of The Wolf. However, Gubbio certainly was plagued by wolves at the time, and in the old town church of San Francesco della Pace, the skeleton of a large wolf was found buried.

Discussion

Having told the story, it would be appropriate to discuss it with the children. What does this tell us about St Francis? How unusual a man was he?

Finally, at the risk of stating the obvious, it would be sensible to warn the children that the story does not mean that they can go up to strange dogs and pat them!

Song: 'Make me a channel of your peace' ('The prayer of St Francis') (C & P 147)

Prayer

A prayer attributed to St Francis of Assisi.

> Lord; make me an instrument of your peace:
> Where there is hatred, let me sow love;
> Where there is injury, pardon;
> Where there is discord, union;
> Where there is doubt, faith;
> Where there is despair, hope;
> Where there is darkness, light;
> Where there is sadness, joy.
> O divine Master,
> grant that I may not so much seek to be consoled as to console;
> to be understood as to understand;
> to be loved as to love;
> for it is in giving that we receive,
> it is in pardoning that we are pardoned,
> and it is in dying that we are born to eternal life.

10.5 ST HUGH OF LINCOLN

Theme A historical figure, Hugh of Lincoln, who most unusually managed to be a prince of the Church, and to retain the common touch. Loved by all, he rebuilt Lincoln Cathedral in the twelfth century after the original Norman building collapsed, and when he died, was canonized as a saint. For centuries thereafter, thousands of pilgrims came every year from all over Europe to pray at his tomb in Lincoln Cathedral.

The story which follows may be read, or could be dramatized using different voices for the people in the crowd, the steward and the bishop.

Story: Hugh of Lincoln

The lanes that criss-crossed the flat fields of Lincolnshire were alive with beetle-like figures hurrying along the roughly rutted tracks towards the city. Some still carried the tools of their trade, a scythe or hoe, or just a staff to lean on. Their clothing was dirty from their

work on the land. Their faces too showed they came straight from their digging or planting or other back-breaking tasks. Here and there a figure would pause to stoop low over an obliging stream and soak his kerchief well in its cool refreshing water. Then, hardly stopping to drink, he would mop his brow and the back of his sun-scorched neck, before hurrying on towards the city and the Bishop's Palace.

Soon the lanes widened into roads that wound steeply upwards into the city's heart. An odd cart or two rumbled slowly along to squeeze a space in the cobbled Palace Square, which was now teeming with jostling peasants, who for one rare day had been allowed to leave their labouring early to come and pay homage to the new Bishop of Lincoln.

'Some say this new bishop is a humble man, living poorly as ourselves,' muttered one fellow in the crowd, his worn face grown old before its time.

'If you believe that, you will believe anything,' scoffed his swarthy companion.

'Even were it true, William,' scowled a third, 'he will soon alter once he has a taste of the power and wealth of being Bishop of Lincoln. Why, he will be the most powerful bishop in all England.'

'That is true,' sighed William, hope draining away from his pinched face. He could not really imagine that King Henry would choose a simple man for such a high position. Suddenly tired, he squatted down on to the cobbles and prepared for a long wait. Soon others followed suit, where room would allow, their ears poised, despite the clamour of the crowd, to listen out for the rumble of carriage wheels.

The new bishop was not far away. Neither was he resplendent in rich robes nor sitting comfortably upon a silken cushion in a sway-

ing carriage. To the chagrin of the churchmen who had come in rich procession, wearing the most extravagant and opulent of robes, to welcome him into the city, their new bishop rode awkwardly upon a mule. Behind him, giving even more offence to these proud men, was a bundle of rough sheepskins tied with simple cord. The churchmen snorted in disgust as they realized that these skins were all the clothes the bishop had brought with him, save the simple monk's habit he wore. He made them feel so ashamed that, when he was not looking, they cut the bundle away, so that it fell by the wayside for some fortunate workman to discover on his homeward journey.

The churchmen were even angrier when Hugh dismounted from the noisy animal and began to make his way through the crowds towards his palace, his feet bare for all to see.

The crowd rose to their feet, oddly silent after the first ripple of surprise. A great feeling of respect went out towards this new bishop, who called himself Hugh. Everything they had heard of him was true. He was dedicated to a life of prayer for his fellow men, rich and poor alike. By living in poverty himself, he was able to show the poor that he felt himself one of them, not far above them in uncaring cruelty.

'You were wrong,' said William to his friends. 'Here amongst us is a true man of God and the people. He will not change.'

'Will he change the emptiness within me?' asked his hungry companion. 'Will he feed my wife and children?'

'Aye,' grunted the third, still unconvinced. 'Will he leave his praying long enough to come out into the streets and fields and do something to help us?'

'We must see how he behaves today,' insisted William. 'Perhaps he will have the scraps thrown out for us to eat. Who knows, but I feel sure he will show us today what kind of bishop he will be.'

Inside the splendid palace, Hugh was not surprised to see that a most extravagant banquet had been prepared for him to share with the rich noblemen who had come to honour him. He summoned his steward and, as the astonished man knelt before him, he spoke simply, 'I desire you to cook three hundred deer.'

'But, Your Grace, is not this food good enough?' spluttered the steward.

'The feast I desire is for the poor of Lincoln, whose hard work in the fields has brought us this food we see before us. Go and prepare for them, so that they may have what they deserve.'

That night, the moon shed its thin light across the fields, as once again the lanes filled with the steady movement of many feet. The feet were of the same simple folk who had entered the city earlier in the day, but the backs were a little straighter and hearts were light. Fathers carried their small children high on their shoulders in a new contentment, come from a feast well enjoyed.

'I wish thee a good night, William,' smiled his swarthy friend. 'From this day forth, our living will not be quite so hard, I be thinking.'

'Aye,' nodded William, warmly, 'for have we not Hugh, Bishop of Lincoln himself, for a true friend?'

Song: 'The building song' (C & P 61)

Leader: St Hugh was also a courageous church leader, and there are many stories of how he stood up to kings and rulers to proclaim the Christian truths of love, justice and mercy.

Prayer

> O God, who endowed your servant Hugh of Lincoln with a wise and cheerful boldness and taught him to commend the discipline of a holy life to earthly rulers: give us grace like him not only to be bold but to

have just cause for boldness, even the fear and love of yourself alone; through Jesus Christ our Lord.

(From *Celebrating Common Prayer*, Mowbray, 1992)

10.6 THE PILGRIM FATHERS

Theme The courage of the Pilgrim Fathers in being prepared to endure the hazards of a ten-week journey across the Atlantic in an old whaling ship, the *Mayflower*, in order to be able to worship God in the way they felt to be right. (Not so much a story, more a historical account retold in an imaginative way.)

Introductory music: *Portsmouth Point* by Walton, or 'Vltava' from *Ma Vlast* by Smetana.

Story: The Pilgrim Fathers

Most of us look forward to travelling to new, exciting surroundings. If our journey takes us across the sea, our sense of adventure is deepened further. Yet, despite the thrill of

seeing strange coastlines and meeting people with vastly differing backgrounds from our own, there is always the desire to return home, back to our family and friends.

How, then, did those Pilgrim Fathers feel in 1620? They took the same journey from the

old familiar world to the challenge of new lands, but they knew, only too well, that they were unlikely to return. Nor could they be sure that they and their families would even reach the new land safely, or would survive a winter in a country unplanted or otherwise prepared for their settlement.

Forget the comfort of today's great ocean liners. Take instead the old whaling ship, the *Mayflower*, with its bare decks and ancient rigging. Squeeze a space for you and your family down below amongst 102 men, women and children. Resign yourself that here you stay for ten long frightening weeks, apart from an occasional walk up on deck, when weather and sickness allow. Comfort yourself with the daily hard biscuit and hunk of well-salted horse meat, as fresh as it could be with no refrigerator on board. The salt makes you thirsty, but go careful with the fresh water – take just a sip or two, for who can say how long the voyage might last?

So your lips get dry and crack a little, and small sores edge your mouth from lack of vitamins. Your body is flea-bitten and you watch the pests hopping about in your blankets, too weak to make the effort of trying to catch them. You long for a wash, but the same bowl gets passed around until its contents are black and you use instead a dampened handkerchief that has caught a few raindrops leaking in after a storm.

The days pass. The ship heaves across the Atlantic and everyone is sick and longing for fresh air. Some brave the strong winds and the rough sailors' curses to totter up on to the rolling deck. Down below, you breathe in the stench of stale vomit on your blankets, the steamy heat of fevered bodies too closely confined and, everywhere, the rank smell of mildew. Occasionally a few peaceful moments of families praying together or singing hymns strengthens you, but then babies wail again, voices rise in anger or distress as men fight to keep their sanity and a precious space for their family.

What was that? A rat scuttles across your feet and gnaws away at the sack of grain you have brought for planting. Can you stand any more? Ten weeks seem endless across a sea that roars and pounds so that the ship groans and creaks and seems certain to break in two and toss you all out into the waiting, devouring waters.

Wait! Someone cries 'Land! Land ahoy!' The ship can stagger into Cape Cod harbour. The voyage is over and there is no going back.

What a way to travel! What a way to choose to travel. Yet it is not fair to suggest that the Pilgrim Fathers chose this voyage, for it was forced upon them. They wanted to worship God in their own way but, at that time, England would not let them. So these sincere people braved the nightmare journey across the sea. Sadly, the harshness of winter in a strange land saw many of them struck down with a terrible sickness. The journey had left them too weak to fight it, and when spring eventually came to soften the earth for seed planting, only fifty people were left alive – only four mothers to care for all the children.

A year after they had landed, the survivors held a feast of Thanksgiving to God, for the Virginian soil was fertile and they were free to worship without punishment. Even today, on the last Thursday in November, the Americans celebrate Thanksgiving Day, in honour of those first brave families.

Song: 'Travel on' (C & P 42) or 'The journey of life' (C & P 45) or 'The pilgrims' hymn' (C & P 146) or 'Waves are beating' (C & P 84)

Prayer

A prayer of St Patrick (adapted).

> May the strength of God pilot us,
> May the power of God preserve us,
> May the wisdom of God instruct us,
> May the hand of God protect us,
> May the way of God direct us,
> May the shield of God defend us.
> May Christ be with us,
> Christ above us
> Christ in us
> Christ before us
> This day and evermore.

11 Using music and dance

Recent years have seen much thought given in schools to the place of music in worship. The emphasis placed by OFSTED on the need for cultural development means that it is now commonplace for a notice to be displayed in the hall giving the details of the piece of music being played on entry and exit from the worship, and the leader of worship will often refer to the music which has been played on entry at the beginning of the worship. An imaginative choice of music to enter to can contribute to the quality of the worship by relating to the theme and setting the tone.

Another major change in recent years has been the variety of songs and hymns for school worship, pitched at the age and ability level of the children. The BBC has been very influential here, with its almost ubiquitous hymn book, *Come and Praise*, linked to its broadcast acts of collective worship; publishers such as A & C Black and Stainer & Bell have also produced some splendid collections of hymns and songs suitable for primary school worship.

In addition to these innovations, however, creative music-making and dance are not often seen in school worship. Often a small primary school will not have a music specialist or someone trained in movement and dance, and in consequence these activities are neglected. The purpose of these exam-

ples is to show that it is possible in worship for a non-specialist to use records or music created by children, incorporating it into story-telling or creating atmosphere and mood; and to illustrate that 'dance' doesn't mean ballet or Morris dancing, but can simply be movement, mime or gesture to act out or represent action in a narrative.

11.1 ANIMALS

This act of worship for Key Stage 1 children was originally part of a wider theme on 'The Earth'. It was set in a classroom which was brightly decorated with children's topic work (art, poetry, papier-maché models) representing many different kinds of animals.

Introductory music: Saint-Saëns, *The Carnival of the Animals*: select and contrast 'Cocks and Hens' and 'Tortoise'.

Ask children what sort of animals they think the music represents, and how these animals move.

Pick children to try and move like these animals.

Play the music again, and let these children move to the music. (The number of children

involved will be dictated by the space available.)

Song: 'The butterfly song' by Brian Howard (JP 94). The song could be illustrated using stick puppets representing the animals referred to in the song, made by the children earlier.

Prayer

> Dear Jesus,
> We love animals!
> The monkey
> the parrot
> the donkey
> the kangaroo
> a dog, a pig, a cat, a horse
> thank you for them all, Jesus.
> Big or small
> fluffy or hairy
> quiet or noisy
> fast or slow.
> Help us to care for them all.

Going-out music: *The Carnival of the Animals*.

II.2 PENTECOST

This act of worship uses recorders, percussion, and children in red costumes representing flames, to dramatize the story of the coming of the Holy Spirit (Acts 2.1-21).

Resources Recording of Falla 'El Amor Brujo' from *Ritual Fire Dance* (Harmonia Mundi, HMD 945213).

Entry music: Recorders playing 'Spirit of God, as strong as the wind' (C & P 63) (tune: 'Skye Boat Song').

Leader: The author of the Book of the Acts of the Apostles was Luke, who had earlier written the Gospel which bears his name, which was all about Jesus. In the Acts of the Apostles, Luke tells us some of the events of the early Church. This is the story of the coming of the Holy Spirit, at the Jewish festival of Weeks or Pentecost. This was fifty days after the festival of Passover, when Jesus had been crucified and had then appeared alive to his disciples.

Reader 1: The disciples were meeting together to celebrate the Feast of Weeks, the Jewish harvest festival.

This was also known as Pentecost, because it took place fifty days after the Passover. They were happy and confident again when they knew Jesus was alive, and Peter was emerging as their natural leader. But so far they had not said anything to anybody outside their own group.

Percussion group: Gradually, starting very quietly, build up a sound of a wind getting up. (Children's own composition, rehearsed previously.)

Reader 2: While they were sitting at table, there was suddenly a sound like a gale force wind through the whole house. As they looked at each other, they saw that every one of them was somehow transformed. When they tried to describe the experience afterwards, they said it looked as if flames of fire were resting on them. It was a tremendous religious experience for all of them. They knew, suddenly, that the Spirit of God which Jesus had promised had come to them. (*Percussion group reaches a climax like a gale force wind*)

Music and dance: To a recording of Falla's 'El Amor Brujo' a group of children dressed in red, to represent flames, move to centre stage and perform a leaping, jumping dance representing flickering flames.

Reader 3: Full of confidence, they went out and began to preach the good news of Jesus Christ to all the pilgrims who were then in Jerusalem.

The sight of the disciples, excited and talkative, rushing out on to the streets and telling every stranger they met about Jesus, amazed the people of Jerusalem. Some said openly that they must be drunk. After one such comment, Peter stood up in the square and spoke to the crowd.

Reader 4: I know what you are saying about us, my friends. But I assure you we are not drunk. What you are seeing today is a fulfilment of the prophet Joel:

The day will come, says your Lord God,

When I will pour out my Spirit on all mankind.

Your sons and daughters shall prophesy,

Old men see dreams, and young men visions,

Even slaves will receive my Spirit.

There will be signs in the sky, and on the earth;

Blood and fire and clouds of smoke.

The sun will go dark, and the moon turn to blood,

Before the great and terrible day of the Lord

Only those who call on the Lord by name will be saved.

My friends, I am speaking to you today about the man Jesus of Nazareth, well known to you all because of his teaching and the marvellous works which God performed through him. You had him crucified, but God raised him to life again, as we can all bear witness. All that you are seeing and hearing now comes from him.

Reader 5: Many of the Jewish people listening to Peter's speech were deeply impressed, and asked Peter what they should do. Peter told them to repent and be baptized, and many people became Christians that day.

Song: 'Spirit of God as strong as the wind' (C & P 63)

Prayer

(From the Holy Communion Service in *The Alternative Service Book 1980*)

Almighty God,
to whom all hearts are open,
all desires known,
and from whom no secrets are hidden:
cleanse the thoughts of our hearts
by the inspiration of your Holy Spirit,
that we may perfectly love you,
and worthily magnify your holy name;
through Christ our Lord. Amen.

Going-out music: 'Les Troubadours du Roi Baudouin', *Missa Luba* (POLY 4268362), a setting of the Mass in traditional Congolese style.

11.3 ASKING GOD FOR HELP

A simple act of worship for Key Stage 1 children, which introduces an aspect of the concept of prayer as asking God for help. The music can be taped or played by the children, depending on the skills available, and the dance is the sort of 'party' dancing that children of this age love doing – they'll need little help from the teacher!

The drama has echoes of the Prodigal Son, but in a simplified form and without the elder brother.

Resources Signpost saying 'Easy Way' and 'Hard Way'. Lighting, to light the 'Easy Way' direction brightly.

Introductory music: 'Watch and pray' (MT).

Leader: Today we are going to think about asking God for help when we are in trouble or difficulty. Jesus said to his followers:

Reader: I say to you, ask, and you will receive; seek, and you will find; knock, and the door will be opened to you (Luke 11.9).

Leader: Some Year Two children have been thinking about what this means. Here are some of their thoughts (*examples*):

Child 1: I think it means, if you ask Jesus to help you, he will.

Child 2: I don't think it means he will help you find something you've lost, like a pen or a book. I think it means, if you've lost your way or can't think what is the right thing to do, and you pray to Jesus, he will help you.

Child 3: When it says, 'Knock and the door will be opened to you,' it's not

really about doors in houses. It's more like opening up the door of your heart, to let Jesus in.

Leader: Here's a story of someone who had a difficult choice to make and rather lost his way.

Enter child dressed as a traveller. Comes to a signpost. One direction says 'Easy Way'; the other says 'Hard Way'. 'Easy Way' is brightly lit; 'Hard Way' is in darkness.

Leader: The traveller, without stopping to think, took the easy way. At first all went well.

Traveller sets off in the 'Easy Way' direction, and comes to a group of children dressed in party clothes. Lights come on, pop music starts, children start dancing. Traveller takes off coat, and joins in.

Leader: But then his money ran out, and his new friends deserted him.

Traveller turns out his pockets, shows they are empty. Others leave, music stops, lights go out.

Leader: He made his way back to the signpost, and sat down, wondering what to do. Then he remembered about asking Jesus for help. Suddenly the hard way didn't seem so difficult after all.

Lights come on in the direction of the 'Hard Way'. Traveller sets off again, this time in the 'Hard Way' direction.

Leader: The right way can seem hard when you're on your own. But with the help of Jesus, we can make it. Shall we say a prayer?

Prayer

Child reads prayer he or she has written, for example:

> Dear Lord, please help us when we have a difficult decision to make. Help us always to choose to do what is right, and if we find it diffi-

cult, help us to do the right thing even if other people laugh at us and say we're silly. Thank you, Lord. Amen.

Song: 'Give me oil in my lamp' (C & P 43)

Going-out music: Britten's ballet, *The Prince of the Pagodas* (the point at which Belle Rose travels through the elements of earth, air, fire and water).

II.4 HANDEL

This is an act of worship which tells the story of the composer George Frederick Handel, and how he had to overcome tremendous difficulties to fulfil his ambition to become a musician. The way in which the story is told uses children who can play keyboard – any level of ability will do! – and whatever combination of instruments the school can put together to represent an orchestra.

Introductory music: Handel, 'Water Music'.

Leader: The music we have been listening to was by a famous composer, George Frederick Handel. This is the story of how George became a musician.

Reader 1: Have your parents made plans for you? Are they dreaming that one day you will be a doctor, or an engineer, a nurse or a famous dress designer? Most of you will develop a special skill or talent you already have waiting inside you, which will probably lead you into careers quite different from those your parents plan for you.

Reader 2: Sometimes children realize they have a special talent even when they are quite small, and this is the story of one small boy who always knew what he wanted to be.

George Frederick Handel's father was an important doctor at the court of the Duke of Saxony in Germany, and he was ambitious for his young son. He dreamed of the day when young George would be a lawyer, so learned that he too would be appointed to the court of the Duke. His son would be the greatest lawyer in the land.

Child dressed as a doctor, with white coat and stethoscope, sits head in hands, dreaming. Boy dressed as a young child sits playing with musical toys.

Reader 1: But as Mr Handel schemed, George played with any musical toy he could find. Angrily, his father burned all of them and filled the nursery with books instead. Then he sent him to school while he was still very young.

The doctor takes the toys away and sits George down at a desk, and makes him read books.

Reader 2: Poor George. Without music he was very unhappy. Music made him come alive. Now his only happiness was at church on Sundays, when he could gaze up at the great organ in the loft and listen to its notes as they whispered or blazed out of the stone pillars. George's Aunt Anna, who took him to church, had been very worried by his pale, miserable face. At church, she began to notice how his face lit up as the organ music flooded the church. He whispered to her that one day he would sit up there and play for God.

Girl dressed as George's aunt comes and takes him by the hand and leads him into a corner of the room or stage made to look like a church pew or chairs. Recording of organ music plays and George looks interested and happy.

Reader 1: The weeks passed into months and George grew more and more unhappy. His mother and Aunt Anna realized that he was pining for music. Then came a wonderful day. It was George's birthday and Aunt Anna crept into his room carrying a very awkward-looking package.

Aunt Anna comes in carrying a portable electronic keyboard in its cardboard box and wrapping paper. She and George unwrap it and plug it in, or switch it on if battery-operated.

Reader 2: It was an old spinet, like a small piano. George was beside himself with joy. Carefully they carried it up into the attic. There they bound the strings with cloth to muffle the sound. Now George could play secretly whenever he wished and his father would not hear him. Night after night, he would creep up into the attic, ignoring the darkness and the cold. Then he would let his fingers run over the keys as they instinctively made music.

George plays the keyboard.

Reader 3: When George was seven years old, his father prepared to visit the court of another Duke. George longed to go too to hear the music he knew would be played for all the visitors. But his father was adamant that George should stay at home and study his school books. This time George did not give in meekly. No sooner had the coach rumbled out through the iron gates of his home, than George began to run stealthily behind it.

George's father, the doctor, takes off his white coat, puts on a smart jacket, and walks off. George runs around the hall as if following the coach. Sound effects of horse walking, if available.

Reader 4: At first he found it quite easy to keep up with the coach as it manoeuvred in the narrow streets, but soon his small legs began to ache. The ground seemed to grow harder by the second and his breath came in deep, rasping gasps as the horses neared open country and began to pick up speed. Bravely George ran on, until finally he had to show himself and the coach was abruptly halted.

George stops. His father comes to him, cross at first, then takes him by the hand.

Reader 3: Young George had come a long way and his father was forced to take him along. It would not do for a doctor to be late when he was the guest of a Duke! George was exhausted but delighted and, once within the court, he spent the days with the orchestra.

School orchestra – any group of instrumentalists, depending on availability – sits rehearsing. George wanders among them and is allowed to try various instruments.

Reader 4: Busy though they were, they could not fail to notice his talent as his fingers stretched out to twang their instruments. Perhaps they mentioned the small boy to their leader, who in turn mentioned him to the Duke. Who knows, but when after the usual Sunday service had

been held in church, George climbed up on to the organ stool and began to play, the Duke himself happened to hear him.

George sits down at the piano and plays. Child dressed as Duke comes and listens, and is impressed. If child playing George is not a pianist, mime and play recording of organ music.

Reader 3: He was so impressed that he urged George's father to recognize that his son was a genius. So at last, George's father acknowledged that his son would not be a famous lawyer, but a mere musician.

George's father takes George by the hand as if taking him home, then sits him down at the piano and gives him some sheet music.

Reader 4: On their return home George was allowed to study his beloved music. Soon, he was composing his own music, conducting his own orchestra and eventually became the court musician, not just for a Duke, but for the Prince of Hanover himself.

George conducts the school orchestra.

Leader: George Frederick Handel was born over 300 years ago, but his music is still being played today throughout the whole world, and especially in churches, for he never forgot his desire to write music for God. His most famous work is his musical story of the life of Jesus, *Messiah*, with its wonderful 'Hallelujah Chorus', still being sung all over the world.

Music: Recorded excerpt from 'Hallelujah Chorus' from Handel's *Messiah*.

Prayer

Reader 1: Let us pray. Let us thank God for George Frederick Handel's courage and determination in becoming a musician.

Reader 2: Let us thank God for George's Aunt Anna, who gave him his first keyboard . . .

Reader 3: . . . and for George's father, who realized that he had been wrong, changed his mind and allowed George to study music.

Reader 4 Let us thank God for George Frederick Handel's genius for music, which we can still enjoy today.

Leader: Now we are going to sing the hymn 'Rejoice the Lord is King!', to a tune written by George Frederick Handel (A & MR 216).

Going-out music: Any music by Handel.

12 Red Letter Days

Most schools celebrate the 'obvious' Christian festivals, Christmas and Easter. Some schools, particularly church schools, also celebrate in worship less popular or well known festivals such as Ash Wednesday, Ascension Day, Whitsun, Advent. There are also many Christian 'occasions' in the calendar which can be the focus of Christian worship in school, such as Christian Aid Week, Mothering Sunday and Christingle. There are also, of course, saints' days: St George, St Patrick, St Valentine, the Patron Saint of your local church.

The purpose of this chapter is not to provide a fully comprehensive list of Red Letter Days

and how to celebrate them; that would require a complete book (and there are already some which attempt to do just that). Rather, this is an attempt to show some examples of different ways in which schools can introduce, and celebrate, Christian Red Letter Days and similar occasions.

Bear in mind that although these occasions are familiar and much-loved milestones in the Christian year to those of us who go to church regularly or who were brought up in the Christian tradition, for many of our children and their parents (and some of our teachers!) they are as strange, unfamiliar, and possibly irrelevant as Diwali or Prophet

Muhammad's birthday. So the starting point really has to be a brief explanation, by the teacher or leader of worship, of what the occasion is, and why it is celebrated at this time in the Christian Church. (I am assuming that if such an occasion is celebrated in school, it will normally be on, or close to, the actual day in the calendar when it is celebrated in church. It's confusing enough for children, what with Jesus being a baby in December and crucified three months later at Easter, without 'doing' other festivals at the wrong time!)

When we celebrate a festival from another faith such as Hinduism, we don't 'pretend' to be Hindus and pray Hindu prayers as if we were Hindus. We would introduce a Hindu prayer with words such as: 'This is a prayer which means a lot to Hindus, and which they would pray in their homes when they celebrate this festival. I am going to read the prayer slowly; you listen carefully, and if you feel you agree with what the prayer is saying, you can say Amen at the end.' Similarly, with a festival from the Christian tradition, we may not be able to assume that the children and adults taking part in the act of collective worship are believers in that tradition, and we may have to use a form of words for introducing prayer which allows all to take part and doesn't exclude non-believers. This will, of course, vary from school to school; aided schools, and sometimes Church of England voluntary controlled schools, may feel freer, because of their school's Trust Deed, to have explicitly Christian worship than would community schools.

Often, the children taking part will have been studying this particular Red Letter Day, and the historical or mythical events that lie behind it, as part of their religious education. This makes it much easier to introduce in worship: 'Year Four have been studying the story of St George – you older boys and girls will probably remember it, and you younger ones will do it when you get to Year Four.'

These occasions can also very appropriately be led by visitors from local churches – and not just the vicar! They could start off by saying something about the regular worship they have in church, and then describe the way in which this particular festival or Red Letter Day is celebrated – the special readings and prayers that are used, the hymns that are sung, the processions, sometimes the special clothes or colour of vestments that are worn, and what this symbolizes.

If the local church is within walking distance, it makes a lot of sense for the collective worship on such days to take place in the church. Then if the building is decorated for a particular festival, such as Harvest Festival or Easter, the children will be able to see it and appreciate it. Sometimes this can work the other way round; if the children have made a display of work on a particular Red Letter Day, this could be displayed in church, and the churchgoers will be able to see it and appreciate it.

12.1 ALL SAINTS' DAY

Resources Music player, overhead projector, song sheet and music, 10–20 candles as appropriate for your children, bucket and sand (for safety). It is a good idea for each candle to be set in a cardboard disc, so that they can be held safely when lit.

Entry music: 'When the saints go marching in' would be quite appropriate.

Leader: Today [or whatever] is All Saints' Day. Can anyone explain what a saint is?

Children may offer: 'someone special', 'a follower of Christ', 'a holy person', etc. Someone may even say, 'We're all saints.'

Leader: Can anyone name a special saint?

Each child who can name a saint is asked if they know who they were or what they did – or the other children can offer information, or the person leading the worship can say. If a name is given that no one knows about, you can either accept it and ask people to investigate, or only choose those who can explain who their saint is (this limits numbers significantly, however). Each child is then called to the front where they receive a candle to hold. (Warn each one firmly about holding it upright and away from body.) Eventually 10 to 20 children are holding lit candles. You will know how many to do; if the level of knowledge is quite low, a smaller number may be better.

Leader: The saints we can name were special people who helped us all to understand God better, and to live a good life. But in fact all the people of the Church are also known as saints. We all learn from each other; indeed, we all learn about God and how to live a good life from every person we meet, whether they are members of the Church or not.

Why is each of these children carrying a candle?

Children may offer: 'to stand for their saint', 'to show the light', 'to be a light' (depending on how much work they have already done on the significance of light).

Leader: Each light represents the light which that saint shone in the world, showing people the way, and helping them to see the great Light which is God.

Prayer

(Spoken by one of the children)

> Lord, we thank you for the people who shine a light in our darkness. Especially we thank you for the saints who showed, and still show us, the way to you.

Usual closing prayer, e.g., The Lord's Prayer.

Conclusion

Children blow candles out gently, and return to their places.

Song: 'Light up the fire' (C & P 55) or 'This little light of mine' (A 14) or 'Give me oil in my lamp' (C & P 43)

Going-out music: Anything suitable, played while children depart.

12.2 CHRISTIAN AID WEEK: BOOKS FOR BOSNIA

The background to this particular act of worship was that the Diocese of Bangor had decided to support Christian Aid Week by making an appeal for books for Bosnia. A teacher from the school had visited Gornji Vakuf, a small town in central Bosnia, and this was known to the children.

If repeated in a different context, this would need to be explained, perhaps with a map to show where Bosnia is, and a brief reminder about the war in Bosnia.

Resources When this was first performed, the teacher who had visited Gornji Vakuf brought in some photographs from his visit.

Reader 1: Before the war Gornji Vakuf was a happy town where Bosnians, Serbs and Croats all lived together in peace. The town had schools, hospitals, offices and many different churches. It was one community. But the war changed everything.

Reader 2: Gornji Vakuf saw three wars. Different armies fought each other and then the people fought each other, neighbour against neighbour. It was terrible. Many people have died, others have moved or been moved.

Reader 3: There is no fighting now but the town is not the same as it was. Most of the buildings have been destroyed. There is no work and it is very difficult moving around the town. It is still dangerous as there are thousands of mines all over the town. Even now one or two people die every month because of an exploding land mine. The town is known as a Highly Dangerous Area.

Reader 4: One girl who lives in Gornji Vakuf is Edina, who is 10 years old. She lives with her mother and brother. She has seen many of her friends and family killed during the war. She has lost four years of her childhood. (*Photographs of Edina are held up*) This is Edina and her family. These photographs are perhaps too small for you to see from the back, but they will be on display in the hall so you can come and look at them later.

Reader 5: Today, Edina attends the Gornji Vakuf Youth House. She can only go to school for three hours a day so there is plenty of time for extra classes at the Youth House. Here she follows activities which help her cope with the effects of the war.

Reader 6: Edina enjoys reading stories and is keen to learn English, but there are very few books and the town library was destroyed in the war. People are now working to build a new library and Youth House as there are many children like Edina who need help.

(When this act of worship was first used, the leader of worship went on to say:

> Our school is helping this effort by collecting money and books to be used in Gornji Vakuf. So please help us; tell all your friends what is needed. The appeal will be running until November, so there is plenty of time. Children like Edina need help. We can give it to them.

Clearly this would need to be modified, depending on the school in which the story is used, and what they are collecting for.)

Song: 'The pollen of peace' (C & P 145)

Prayer

Leader: Listen to this prayer from Bosnia, and if you feel you are able to, say 'Amen' at the end.

Dear Lord, Father of peace
Lead me from death to life
From lies to truth.

Lead me from hopelessness to hope
From fear to faith.

Lead me from hate to love
From war to peace.

Let peace fill our hearts, our world, our universe. Amen.

12.3 ADVENT

Age range: Key Stage 1

Resources Tie seven or eight silk scarves together so that they are in a long string. Push them into a jacket sleeve and leave dangling, but hidden inside. Wear the jacket, with one scarf showing from the sleeve. Have three cards saying the following in nice large print, big enough to be read from the back of the hall:

● Christmas is all about Jesus.

● Jesus was born to show us that God loves us.

● God's love never ends.

Introductory music: *Fantasia on Christmas Carols* by Vaughan Williams.

Leader: Talk to the children about what they think Christmas is all about (e.g. presents, turkey, decorations, tree, etc.). Introduce card 1, 'Christmas is all about Jesus' (*two children to hold it up*).

Ask the children why they think Jesus was born. After listening to their ideas, introduce card 2, 'Jesus was born to show us God's love'.

Ask the children if they can think of any words that might describe God's love (e.g. deep, long, all around, never-ending, etc.). Bring their focus to the jacket. Say 'Oh dear, it looks as if something is wrong with my jacket. Could somebody come and pull this handkerchief?' One child pulls all the scarves out. (*Allow the children to squeal with delight!*)

Reiterate that God's love is long. Tie the two ends of the line of scarves together to make a circle. Turn the circle round and round through your hands and keep saying 'God's love goes on and on'. Introduce card 3, 'God's love never ends'. Focus on all three cards and read them through, all together.

Song: 'God's love is like a circle' (source unknown; sing to the tune of 'Puff the Magic Dragon'):

God's love is like a circle,
A circle big and round,
And when you have a circle,
No ending can be found,
And so the love of Jesus
Goes on eternally,
Forever and forever,
I know that God loves me.

All of the children can join hands, preferably in a circle, or make a wide circle shape with their arms.

Prayer

Dear Father, we know that your love is like a circle and that it goes on and on and never ends. As Christmas approaches, we are reminded that Jesus came into the world to show us just how much you love us. Thank you, dear Lord. Amen.

Concluding music: *Fantasia on Christmas Carols* by Vaughan Williams.

12.4 ADVENT

Age range: Key Stage 2

Resources Advent ring with five candles.

Entry music: 'Sanctus' from Fauré's *Requiem*.

Song: 'The candle song' (MWS)

Leader: I wonder if anyone can tell me what was special about last Sunday?

(Hopefully, someone will know it was Advent Sunday!)

Yes, it was Advent Sunday, the beginning of the Church's year and the beginning of the special time which leads up to Christmas. The word Advent means 'coming' and it is the time when we prepare ourselves for the birth of Jesus. The shops begin to get ready for Christmas very early and sometimes people get so excited about buying presents and food and sending cards that the real meaning of Christmas, Jesus coming into our world, is forgotten. How could we prepare for Jesus' birth?

Children's answers may include: In our prayers, reading about the birth of Jesus, our school play, helping others who won't have a place to stay or good things to eat, etc. If answers are slow in coming, leader may need to prompt.

Leader: Today we have a special Advent ring. Do you know why we have five candles on the ring? *(Some may know. After fielding replies, leader summarizes)* Yes, there is one for each Sunday in Advent and the fifth candle is for Christmas Day. We light one on the first Sunday in Advent, two on the second Sunday, and so on until Christmas Day, when we light all five. Why are candles special when we think about Jesus? *(After replies, leader summarizes)* Jesus is the Light of the World, bringing peace and hope to us all at Christmas. Today we are going to light our first candle and then think quietly about how we can prepare for the coming of Jesus. *(The first candle is lit)*

Prayer

Father we thank you for the gift of your Son at Christmas. As we light our Advent candle today, we remember all those people in the world who do not have enough to eat or a warm place to stay. *(Short pause for silent prayer)* Thank you for our homes and families and all your special gifts to us. Amen.

Song: 'Jesus your light is shining within us' (MT)

12.5 EPIPHANY

This could be the first assembly of Spring Term, if the children have already heard the Singing Shepherd story. If not, read or paraphrase the story before going on from Discussion 1 below (*The Singing Shepherd* by Angela Elwell Hunt, Lion Picture Stories, 1992).

Resources Overhead projector, song sheet and music, three candles lit. Large Christmas card with three wise men shown in picture.

Introductory music: 'Three kings from Persian lands afar' (*Christmas Night – Carols of the Nativity*. Cambridge Singers, Cond. John Rutter, COLC 106).

Introduction

Draw attention to the three candles. Either have a question and answer session drawing on story, *The Singing Shepherd*, if this was read to whole school during the final assembly of preceding term, or tell the story. Try to elicit who helped the boy find the baby Jesus, and how he went home from his adventure the same, but completely different.

Discussion 1

Draw attention back to the three candles and explain that these stand for three wise men. What do you think 'wise' means? Children may offer: 'clever', 'knows a lot', etc. Make connection with the ability to use knowledge.

Discussion 2

Briefly tell the story of the three wise men (Matthew 2.1-12). Show Christmas card with three wise men on it. Artists show them very differently – look particularly at the expression on their faces. (It may be possible, if this was prepared before Christmas, for the children to bring in a range of Christmas cards showing the three wise men, and a display of these to be made up.)

Leader: They had been used to being really important among adults, yet they had come miles and miles to see a baby – why?

Children may offer: 'he was special', 'they thought he was the King'.

Explain the meaning of 'epiphany' – manifestation, or sudden recognition of God in our own lives – usually associated with change.

Leader: The three wise men went home completely changed. We also use the word 'epiphany' for moments in our lives when we hear or see or understand something that changes everything completely for us.

One truly new thing for the wise men and for the people who became Christians thereafter was to see children as very important. The Romans treated them as things to be bought or sold – not as people to be cared for and listened to. Jesus taught how important children were. This meant a sea-change of attitude – and it is one of the reasons why Christmas is really a children's festival.

Prayer

Lord, help us to treasure those moments when we see everything differently, to look out for them and be ready to change.

Lord, help us to use what we know for good. As the wise men did, help us to search you out and be prepared to go home completely changed.

Closing prayer (whichever prayer is normally used).

Blow out candles.

Song: 'We three kings' (MP 740) or 'Wake up each day' (A 60) – especially if it is first day of term. See if any child can remember the 'long word', 'epiphany'.

Going-out music: 'Three kings from Persian lands afar'.

12.6 ST MARTIN'S DAY/ ARMISTICE DAY

This is an assembly for 11 November (Armistice Day) which links with the celebration of St Martin – 11 November is also St Martin's Day.

Introductory music: 'Evacuee' by Enya (*Shepherd's Moon* WEA 9031).

Resources   A large cloak. A picture of a Roman soldier – better still an example of

Roman armour. This can be borrowed from a museum/costume shop.

Leader: This morning we are celebrating St Martin's Day. Martin was a Roman soldier. He'd heard about Christianity, but he wasn't a Christian. Roman soldiers were disciplined, hard, resourceful, etc. (*Leader ad libs on this*) They'd wear their cloaks when it was cold, and they'd wrap themselves up in their cloaks to sleep at night.

One day Martin was riding through France. It was a bitterly cold day and a harsh wind was blowing snow in gusts around him. As he rode up to the gates of the city, a poor beggar lying by the side of the road lifted up his arms to beg for money or food. 'Have pity on me, Roman soldier!' he called.

The other soldiers with Martin laughed and rode on ahead but something about the beggar made Martin stop.

'I have nothing to give you,' Martin shouted into the fierce wind. Then looking at the beggar shaking and shivering, he took his red soldier's cloak from his shoulders and, drawing his sword, he cut the cloak in two and gave half to the beggar. The beggar looked up into Martin's face and thanked him for the warm gift. It was a look that Martin was never to forget.

That night, shivering in what was left of his cloak, Martin had a dream. In the dream Martin saw the figure of Jesus, and when Martin saw his face he recognized the face as that of the beggar. But what shocked Martin most was that Jesus was wearing half of a soldier's cloak – Martin's cloak, the piece he had given to the beggar.

That day Martin became a Christian – a soldier of Christ.

Prayer

The assembly could end here with a prayer, e.g.:

Jesus, friend of the friendless; helper of the poor; healer of the sick;
    Whose life was spent in doing good: let us follow in your footsteps.
Make us strong to do right; gentle with the weak; and kind to all who are in sorrow;
That we may be like you, our Lord and Master. Amen.

Alternatively, Martin's sacrifice could be linked to the sacrifice of soldiers in war. Many of them also gave up something that was precious to them – their lives.

Taking part in the two minutes' silence at 11.00am could strengthen this imagery still further, particularly if the service was timed to coincide with the national observance.

Prayer

A suitable prayer at this point could be:

Teach us, Father, how terrible war is. Teach us first to keep peace in our own homes and then to work for peace in the world. Help us to remember the courage of those soldiers who fought so that we might live our lives in peace. Many gave their most precious gift, the gift of their lives. Amen.

If conditions allow, local ex-soldiers and members of the British Legion could be invited to attend, and poppies could be 'on sale', etc.

13 Using visitors

Most schools invite people in to lead collective worship from time to time. Some have a list of visitors who come in regularly. Often the list includes local clergy and ministers. This chapter looks at the kinds of people who might be encouraged to visit to lead collective worship; the sort of preparatory information you should give to visitors; and how to help visitors to get better at leading worship with children. By its nature, this chapter does not really lend itself to examples of acts of worship led by visitors that could be reproduced by others, but a couple of examples are given that schools – and visitors! – might find interesting and helpful.

First, who might usefully be invited in to lead worship? Many people feel that they cannot

lead worship; that this is only for ordained clergy and ministers. This attitude is changing as lay leadership of worship increasingly becomes the norm in churches, and potential visitors need to be reassured that they are not required to celebrate the Eucharist! There are basically two things you could ask a visitor to do: to speak during an act of worship, and to lead the act of worship. These two functions are different and you need to be clear when making the invitation exactly what it is for. The first category, to speak during an act of worship, opens the field, as it were, to almost anybody who has something interesting or valuable to say. How widely you look for visiting speakers in this category will depend on your school policy for collec-

tive worship. A broad policy, which sees worship as 'worth-ship', celebrating matters of shared value and worth, would enable you to have acts of worship on topics such as caring for those in need (the blind, the elderly, the handicapped), looking after the environment, etc., and to invite in speakers who are committed to meeting need from an altruistic, moral or social standpoint, without necessarily being Christian themselves.

A narrower policy, which defines school worship in more specifically Christian terms, may mean that you restrict those whom you invite to speak in worship to people who are themselves committed Christians. It is worth noting, however, that this can still be a very broad field of potential speakers, from interesting people in your own parish who visit the elderly, organize Christian Aid Week collections, collect for LEPRA, edit and collate the parish newsletter, etc., through to internationally known speakers who just happen to be in the locality and might be persuaded to come and speak to children for ten minutes.

Two cautionary notes regarding speakers from charities and churches. If the speaker is from a charity, do be clear whether or not his/her visit is in connection with fundraising by or in the school. If you just want the visitor to speak about guide dogs for the blind, but not to seek to raise funds because you have decided to support other charities this year, do say so. Secondly, if your visitor is from a church, do explain very carefully that you are inviting him/her to speak on a particular topic but not to evangelize. Most Christian visitors to schools do understand this, but some can get a bit carried away!

The second category of visitors, those who come to lead the whole act of worship, will normally be professionals who are experienced in leading worship, but not necessarily ordained. Local priests and ministers, of course; lay readers and others trained in leading worship; specialists such as Diocesan Education team personnel, youth and children's workers or advisers; staff from the local secondary school who lead collec-

tive worship. There are two things to bear in mind here. First, such people may be used to leading worship with committed Christian groups; you may need to remind them that a school is not a church – they cannot assume Christian commitment on the part of those present, and some Christian concepts which they as Christians take for granted, e.g. grace and forgiveness, may not be familiar to all the children. Secondly, these visitors may be used to speaking to, and leading worship for, adults. They may need help in keeping the language simple, especially for Key Stage 1 children. If the visitor is to lead the whole act of worship, it may be best if the Head (or co-ordinator of collective worship) and the visitor plan the service together.

PREPARATORY INFORMATION FOR NEW VISITORS

You may find it helpful to prepare an information sheet for visitors coming to speak at, or lead, collective worship. This might include:

- A summary of your policy for collective worship.

- Your programme of topics for the term, and whether the visitor is expected to conform to this.

- If it is a 'one-off' visit on a special day, e.g. a saint's day, whether or not this topic will have been addressed earlier in the week.

- The hymn, whether in books or OHP: is this to be chosen by visitor or school?

- Likewise music before the service: does the school choose it? If so, let the visitor know what it will be.

- The 'style' used for prayers/readings. Will the visitor expect children to do readings/lead prayers? If so, preparation beforehand will be needed.

- The version of the Lord's Prayer that is used.

- The way in which prayer is usually introduced (e.g. 'I am going to read a prayer from . . . Please listen carefully and if you wish, make the prayer your own by saying Amen').

- Whether the visitor will be introduced and if so, by whom.

- Whether the visitor will have time for an informal chat afterwards with the children.

- The length of time available for the talk/service.

Less easy to put on a checklist is the question of language. Do discuss with the visitor the age group to be present, and the vocabulary and concepts that will be appropriate.

Another tricky area is questions. Speakers often want to ask the children questions, and of course this is a good way of keeping the children involved and interested. Do explain, however, especially to new visitors who are not used to children, that the little ones will put their hands up to any question (but may not have anything relevant to say), and that in a big hall, the older ones at the back may not be easily heard. It is often a good idea to suggest to the speaker that he/she lets you pick the children to answer the questions. You may also have to remind the visitor that, even if the answer is not what they wanted or expected, he/she should acknowledge it before going on to another child, and not just say 'No'!

HOW TO HELP VISITORS TO IMPROVE

This is the most difficult area of all. If the speaker is to be a regular visitor to the school, and really isn't very good at speaking to children, you do have to try and help. How you do this is going to vary according to circumstances and personalities; you may be able to go for a direct approach and gently point out after the act of worship that words like 'resurrection' and 'parousia' are a bit hard for five-year-olds! Or you may invite

the visitor to come to one of the acts of worship which you lead, and explain to him/her beforehand how you propose to deal with those aspects which you think he/she has difficulty with. Another approach is to have a meeting of several members of staff who lead worship, to review several different acts of worship in order to decide what is working well and what could be improved, and invite the visiting speaker to join you. The important thing is to tackle the problem straight away, and not to let it drag on and grumble about it behind the visitor's back.

13.1 SISTER GEMMA'S VISIT

This is one of a series of acts of worship led by people who have given their lives to the service of God. It is, quite simply, how Sister Gemma led the worship, and what she said. Obviously, no one else could use this material directly! But you might find this useful to show to new or potential visitors as an example of how to go about it, the kind of language to use, how to involve the children, and so on.

Resources Music player, overhead projector, song sheet and music, candle and matches.

Music for entry and exit: To set mood – very tempting to suggest 'Dominique' by the Singing Nun, but plainsong chanting would be more appropriate.

Sister Gemma: Hands up who has a sister I bet you sometimes get on well with your sister but sometimes you argue, or even fight? But if someone were to threaten you or upset you, your sister would be right there defending you – she'd be on your side. Well, that's the kind of sister I am. There are some people who decide that what they want to do with their lives is to be a sister or brother to everyone they meet, to be on their side. They call themselves monks (the men) and nuns (the women).

Theme 1: Clothes

Sister Gemma: Has anyone seen any films about nuns?

Children offer: *Sister Act, Nuns on the Run.*

Sister Gemma: What did you notice about the nuns in that film?

Children offer: 'They were men.'

Siste Gemma: That's true, they were men, and they were robbers, weren't they? But how did you know they were pretending to be nuns?

Children offer: 'They wore special clothes.'

Sister Gemma: That's right, and many years ago I also wore all those special clothes that covered me up, but now my group of nuns has decided that we should look just like other people, so that we can be part of the community we are working for.

Theme 2: History of IBVM

Sister Gemma: Some of you have been studying the Tudors. In that time there wasn't any girl power, and if you were a girl you were not allowed to go to school or learn anything so that you couldn't really do anything serious. What do you learn in school?

Children offer: 'Maths, reading, painting,' etc.

Sister Gemma: Well, in those days if you were a girl, you couldn't learn to do any of those things. Now, there was a woman called Mary who thought that was wrong, and got together with some women friends to start a school for girls. People thought she was doing a bad thing and they put her in prison, but her friends kept going, and now there are people like me all over the world working to do as Mary did, and be on the side of girls and boys so that they can go to a good school and learn all the things that you enjoy learning.

Prayer

God, I thank you that there are people who are on my side. I thank you for my brothers and sisters who look after me. Help us all to be a loving, caring brother or sister to everyone we meet today, and use our power for good. We ask this, trusting in your everlasting love. Amen.

Song: 'One more step' (C & P 47)

Check understanding of main issues.

13.2 THE BABY

Age range: Key Stage 1

A mother brings her four-week-old baby into school, as part of the preparation for Christmas.

Resources Large-scale nativity scene – perhaps painted by children as a backdrop. Full size 'manger' prepared as a crib.

Introductory music: 'Mary had a baby', or other suitable nativity carol.

Announce that today there is to be a very special visitor. The visiting 'mum' comes in, carrying the baby or wheeling the pram (or is already seated at the front with the leader of worship, according to preference).

Ask the children what they think the little baby needs. (Draw out responses such as warmth, food, care, love.) As each need is expressed, the leader of worship asks the mother to show the children, and tell them, how she cares for that aspect of the baby's needs. Most mums who are brave enough to come into school in this way will be able to explain and show quite simply what they do.

Ask the children to think about the baby; how helpless he is, how vulnerable; and draw comparisons with the baby Jesus, and how he too was a helpless baby who had to be looked after by his mother Mary, in difficult circumstances when they couldn't even find a hotel room.

The baby, wrapped up in warm clothing (not too much, if the school is warmly heated!) is then placed carefully in the ready-prepared 'manger' crib, and all sing 'Away in a manger'.

Reflective prayer

Invite the children to think about themselves as babies, and how they were cared for; babies they know, perhaps in their own family, and how they help care for them; babies in parts of the world who are undernourished because of famine or war; and finally, to think once again of Jesus coming into the world as a helpless and homeless baby.

Song: 'Hush little baby' (A 63)

Going out: The children could file quietly past the sleeping (or crying!) baby in the manger on their way out.

14 Developing a theme

Often a topic or theme is too broad to be covered in one act of worship; instead, it could be cumulatively developed over several days, or perhaps once a week over several weeks. This can have the effect of heightening expectancy, particularly if it is a story which the children don't know and which leads up to an exciting climax. An example of this is the story of Esther.

Another example is where the topic can be unpeeled, layer by layer, like an onion. The theme 'Looking at ourselves' is one of these; starting with wrapped packages, where you can't tell what's inside; going on to people, when you can sometimes tell what they are like, or the mood they're in, from the expres-

sion on their faces; and finally trying to work out what someone is worth.

A third example is where the topic naturally breaks down into three or more components, each of which lends itself to a complete act of worship. The theme 'People who help us' starts with people who help us in everyday life; goes on to people who help us in school; then turns the idea round to how we (i.e. the children) can help others. This example is given in outline.

Some dos and don'ts:

- Do recap each successive day, to remind the children where you've got to in the sequence or story.

- Do summarize at the end of the sequence, to remind the children of the whole story or topic.

- Do think carefully whether the link between each individual component of the series is obvious, or needs to be emphasized.

- If different people are to be involved, do liaise with each other to ensure continuity, and do refer to what the previous speaker was saying or doing.

- Don't have too big a gap between episodes; one a week is just about okay, but a week is a very long time in the life of a small child.

- Don't carry the sequence on too long; you want the children to come in breathlessly expectant, not thinking 'Oh good grief, not Paul's Travels again.' 'Esther' in three episodes is probably okay, but *The Lion, the Witch and the Wardrobe* spread out over a term is probably too much.

- Don't forget you've started a series! There's a group of children in a Lincolnshire school who think the Lord's Prayer is 'Our Father who art in heaven', because the vicar started to teach them what it meant phrase by phrase in his weekly assemblies but forgot after the first two episodes.

14.1 ESTHER AND MORDECAI

Background for the teacher: The story of Esther was written between 150 and 100 BC. It is set in Persia in the reign of King Ahasuerus, or Xerxes, approximately 400 years before. It is a novel, written to explain the festival of Purim, which some Jews living in the East had adopted as a kind of carnival. The name Mordecai represents Marduk, the chief Babylonian god, and Esther stands for Ishtar, the Babylonian goddess.

It is quite possible that the story originated in Persis, where the followers of the Persian religion Zoroastrianism were fanatical and

persecuting non-believers at this time. They may well have persecuted the Jews.

Episode One

Leader: Explain something of the background to the novel, from the above information, and that the story will be told in three episodes.

Once upon a time, in the reign of King Xerxes, there was a great banquet given in the royal palace to which all the important people of the land were invited. The wine flowed so freely that Queen Vashti, the wife of Xerxes, decided that it would be more proper for the ladies to have their banquet separately. So she and all the ladies retired to the queen's apartments, where no doubt they had plenty of wine to drink as well.

The feast went on for seven days, at the end of which King Xerxes was quite drunk. He sent his servants to Queen Vashti's apartments, telling her to put on her royal robes and crown and come out to him. She was famous for her beauty, and Xerxes wanted to show her off to his guests.

To his great surprise and annoyance, Queen Vashti refused to come out. Perhaps she thought they were all drunk and would insult her; whatever the reason, she sent the servants back and stayed in her apartment.

'Won't come?' roared the king. 'What does she mean by it? Am I not the king of all Persia, from Ethiopia to India? How dare she!'

Xerxes sent for his closest advisers, and asked them what he should do. They consulted together, then the chief minister gave the king their considered opinion.

'Queen Vashti has done wrong in disobeying you, your majesty,' he said. 'Her action is made worse by the fact that all the women have seen and heard her. If she gets away with it, things will never be the same again. All the women-folk will start disobeying their husbands, and then where would we be? It would mean the breakdown of society.'

'Well, I can quite see that!' the king exploded. 'I shall be a laughing stock! But what can I do about it?'

'Let it be known that Queen Vashti is in disgrace, and that she is never to enter your court again,' the chief minister advised. 'Then pick another queen.'

The king stared at him, and slowly began to smile.

'An excellent idea!' he said. 'And how do you suggest I pick another queen?'

The chief minister cleared his throat. 'We suggest you have a competition, your majesty,' he said.

'A competition?' asked the king, puzzled.

'Yes, your majesty. A kind of – ah – beauty competition. Appoint officers in all your provinces to pick out the most beautiful young women they can find, to be brought before you. You – ah – inspect them, and pick the most beautiful.'

The king roared with laughter, and appointed the officers to make the selection at once. The next twelve months were one long beauty parade. Xerxes did nothing by halves. Beautiful girls came from all over the empire to the royal palace in Susa, spent weeks preparing themselves, and then paraded before the king.

To be continued!

Leader: Draw out one or two key points from the narrative. What does this episode tell you about society's attitude to women at the time? How does it compare with today? Was Xerxes fair to Queen Vashti?

Song: This topic lends itself to a short, very general hymn or song which can be sung in each episode for continuity; such as 'Rejoice in the Lord always' (C & P 95).

Reflective prayer

Lord, help us to think about our attitude towards other people. Help us to be respectful and considerate towards everyone we meet – rich or poor, young or old, ugly or beautiful, male or female; and to look for the best in everybody.

Episode Two

Leader: Remind the children of the key points in the previous episode: how Queen Vashti offended the king, the chief minister's advice, and the beauty parade to pick another queen.

One of the king's courtiers was a Jew named Mordecai, who had been brought into exile by Nebuchadnezzar. He had a beautiful adopted daughter called Esther, and she was taken to the palace to prepare for the competition. Mordecai used to walk by the women's quarters every day, to make sure she was all right.

'Now remember, Esther,' he said to her, 'whatever you do, don't admit you are Jewish. We Jews are not popular, and it would spoil your chances.'

When it came to Esther's turn to appear before the king, Xerxes was quite captivated by her. He picked her out of the line-up and sat her down next to him. When he found she was as witty and charming as she was beautiful, Xerxes made up his mind.

'That's it!' he told the officials. 'Send the other girls away, and announce that Esther is queen.'

There was a great celebration, a public holiday was declared, and Esther was made queen. But she never told Xerxes anything about her background.

One day Mordecai was in court going about his duties when he overheard two of the king's attendants plotting to kill the king. Mordecai went at once to Queen Esther, and told her all he had overheard. She reported it to the king and the matter was investigated at once. The attendants were hanged and the king asked Queen Esther where she had first heard of the plot.

'Your loyal servant Mordecai reported it to me, sire,' Esther replied.

Xerxes was very pleased with Mordecai and entered his name in the court chronicle.

The chief steward in the palace at this time, a man of great influence, was called Haman. He had a very inflated idea of his own importance and used to make all the other court officials bow down to him whenever he passed. Mordecai, being Jewish, would have none of this.

'The only one I bow down to is my God,' he told Haman.

Haman was furious and, when he realized that Mordecai was a Jew, his anger turned into hatred for all the Jewish race. He made a plan and went to King Xerxes.

'Your majesty,' he said, 'there is a group of trouble-makers in your empire, who refuse to obey your laws. It is an insult to you to permit them to live.'

'By heaven, you're right!' Xerxes exclaimed. 'Who are these rogues?'

'They call themselves Jews, your majesty,' Haman replied. 'If you will write out an order for their removal, I shall see that it is carried out.'

Xerxes wrote the decree at once, ordering that all the Jews in the empire were to be killed. Haman had copies of the decree sent out to the governors of all the provinces and sat back rubbing his hands in glee.

When Mordecai heard about it, he tore his clothes, put on sackcloth, and poured ashes on his head as a sign of mourning. Esther heard that he was walking about the palace like this and sent for him at once.

'What on earth are you up to, Mordecai?' she exclaimed. 'You know that mourning is not allowed in the palace!'

'Haven't you heard about the king's decree?' Mordecai asked.

Esther shook her head, and Mordecai told her all about Haman's plot.

'That's awful!' exclaimed Esther. 'But what can I do? I dare not go to the king unless he sends for me first.'

Mordecai looked at her grimly.

'Don't imagine that Haman will let you escape,' he said. 'Remember, you're Jewish too. Someone is bound to give you away.'

Esther thought hard.

'There may be a way,' she said. 'Leave it to me.'

To be continued!

Leader: Emphasize the key points in the narrative. Was Mordecai just using Esther's beauty, or did he feel he was doing the best thing for her by entering her for the competition? Why did Esther conceal the fact that she was Jewish? What sort of a man was Mordecai? (Loyal to the king, loyal to his Jewish background, prepared to stand up for his faith.) And Haman? (Selfish, vain, cunning, evil.)

Song: As Episode One.

Reflective prayer

Lord, help us, when we encounter wrongdoing, to take the right course of action as Mordecai did; and if people offend our dignity,

help us to take it calmly and not get puffed up with a sense of our own importance like Haman.

Episode Three

Leader: Again remind the children of the key points so far: how Esther came to be queen, Mordecai's loyalty, Haman's anger, and how he looked for a way to blame the Jews for something they hadn't done, so that he could get rid of them.

Mordecai had just told Esther about Haman's plot. Esther put on her royal robes, and went to stand by the gateway to the inner court, where the king was sitting. Xerxes was in a good mood that day, and when he saw Esther, he called her in.

'What can I do for you, Esther?' he said. 'Anything you like – just ask.'

Esther curtsied.

'If it please your majesty,' she said, 'I should like to invite you and your chief steward Haman to come to dinner in my apartment tonight.'

The king agreed readily, and that night Esther tried to find an opportunity to get him to see what Haman was doing. But the king refused to talk about court affairs over his meal and in desperation, Esther asked them both to come to dinner again the following night. Wanting to please her, the king agreed, and Haman was very flattered.

On his way home that night, Haman passed Mordecai, who again would not bow to him. Seething with rage, he ordered a scaffold to be built the very next day, so that Mordecai could be hanged.

That night the king couldn't sleep. He sent his attendant to fetch the court chronicle to be read to him; that usually sent him to sleep. When the attendant came to the bit about Mordecai foiling the plot to kill the king, Xerxes sat up.

'I remember that!' he exclaimed. 'Did we ever give Mordecai any reward?'

'I don't believe we did, sire,' the attendant replied.

Just then they heard voices in the courtyard outside. It was Haman, showing the carpenters where he wanted the scaffold to be built.

'Come in, Haman!' called the king. 'Tell me, if there is someone I wish to honour, what ought I to do?'

Haman thought the king must mean him. Who else would Xerxes want to honour but his chief steward? He thought hard, then chose the honour that he wanted most of all.

'I think that man should be dressed in royal robes and put on one of the royal horses,' Haman said. 'Then he should be led through the streets of the city, while officers of the court shout, "This is how the king honours his servant!"'

'Yes, I think that would do very well,' said the king. 'See to it, will you? Mordecai the Jew is the man I want to reward.'

Then he yawned and waved Haman out of the room.

Haman could hardly contain himself. Mordecai, of all people! But there was no way out – he would have to obey the king's orders.

Next day, to Mordecai's astonishment, he found himself dressed in royal robes, seated on a magnificent horse and being taken in triumph through the city. 'This is the man the king wishes to honour,' Haman hissed through gritted teeth as he led the procession.

That night, the king went again with Haman to dine with Queen Esther. At the end of the meal, the king pushed back his chair and smiled at his beautiful young wife.

'Ask anything you like, my dear, and you shall have it,' he said.

Esther saw her chance.

'My lord, I ask that you should save the lives of myself and my people. We have been condemned to death by a wicked and unjust man.'

Haman began to squirm uneasily in his seat. He didn't like the way the conversation was going at all.

'What do you mean?' asked the king hotly. 'Who can possibly have condemned you to death?'

Esther pointed at Haman.

'That is the man,' she said. 'Haman, who has falsely accused my people the Jews of disloyalty to you, the king.'

The king was so angry he couldn't trust himself to speak. He strode out of the apartment and began pacing up and down outside.

Haman fell to his knees and began pleading with Esther for his life. In his despair, he seized hold of the hem of her skirt just as the king came back into the room.

'Are you going to assault the queen while I am still here?' Xerxes shouted. He flung the terrified Haman across the room and turned to his attendants, who had come in to see what was happening.

'What am I to do with a man who tries to kill my wife?' he shouted.

The attendant took the question seriously.

'Haman has had a scaffold built in the palace yard,' he said. 'He was going to have Mordecai hanged from it.'

'Just the thing!' the king exclaimed.

He ordered Haman to be hanged from his own scaffold and appointed Mordecai as chief steward in his place. Queen Esther announced that a festival would be held to celebrate the escape of the Jews from Haman's evil plot. This festival, Purim, is still celebrated today.

Leader: Draw out the key points: Esther's cleverness and courage, the king's readiness to see reason and act justly and fairly and, most important of all, the reason why the story was written, the unfair way in which Jews down the centuries have been blamed and made scapegoats for the wrongs in society. (The extent to which this is drawn out will depend upon the age and background of the children, and whether there is to be follow-up in class, e.g. on the Holocaust.)

Song: As Episode One.

Reflective prayer

Lord, help us to be as clever and brave as Esther, as ready to take the right action as the king, and never to let hatred and prejudice govern our lives as Haman did. Amen.

14.2 LOOKING AT OURSELVES

Three separate, but related, acts of worship.

1 It's what's inside that counts

Resources Two pre-wrapped parcels; one is bigger and wrapped in bright and colourful paper with a big bow. The second is smaller and wrapped in brown crumpled paper, with Sellotape.

Leader: Who likes getting presents? When might you get presents?

Children: Suggest various times: birthdays, Christmas, Easter, anniversaries, when a relative comes to stay, passing exams, etc.

Leader: Bring out the two boxes that are already wrapped. Choose two children to come out and handle each of the presents.

Ask them to describe how heavy the presents feel, etc. and to guess what might be inside. Compare the two on a chart, e.g.:

BIG	SMALLER
looks bright and colourful	tatty brown paper
heavy	light
makes a noise	very light sound

Leader: I wonder which present you would like if you had the choice? What could they be?

Ask the children to choose. Then ask them to open the present. First the big, grand-looking one – inside could be a brick, rubble, stones, etc. The second present could contain a balloon/small packet of marshmallows/bubbles, anything simple that the children would like.

Leader: We have to try and be careful not to be full of things that are heavy and rubbish and not very useful to ourselves or others. We can all choose the way we react and talk to each other. The most important thing to remember is that God knows what we are like. He can see inside us and knows whether we are full of rubbish and what we are thinking. But most important of all he loves us and wants us all to be full of good things on the inside as well as the outside.

Prayer

Either Prayer 1:

God be in my head
And in my understanding.
God be in my eyes
And in my looking.
God be in my mouth
And in my speaking.
God be in my heart
And in my thinking.
God be at my end
And at my departing.

From a Book of Hours, 1514

Or Prayer 2:

Dear heavenly Father, we know that you love each one of us and we ask that you will help us to become more like Jesus every day.

Hymn: 'Jesus' hands were kind hands' (SSL 33)

2 Your thoughts show on the outside

Resources   Six large pieces of card, each with a 'mood' written on. Book: *The Twits* by Roald Dahl (Puffin, 1982).

It is often a good idea to use books that the children know and enjoy to illustrate something you are trying to explain. In this case, the book is *The Twits* by Roald Dahl.

Begin by giving six children each a card on which a number of moods are written which they have to mime, e.g. happy, sad, bad tempered, excited, thoughtful, nervous, etc.

Each takes a turn and the rest of the children guess what it is they are portraying.

Leader: Have you ever noticed that the way you are feeling on the inside always seems to show on your face? As teachers we can often tell whether you are listening or concentrating just by looking at your faces.

How many of you have read or heard about Mr and Mrs Twit? Were they very nice people to know? Would you like to live next door to them? The amazing thing is that Mrs Twit wasn't always as horrible as she is in the book. No, in fact this is what it says (*read extract*).

So you make sure that you don't end up by being like Mrs Twit. Think nice thoughts and let what's on the inside shine through to the outside.

Prayer

Either Prayer 1:

Lord of the loving heart,
May ours be loving too.
Lord of the gentle hands,
May ours be gentle too.
Lord of the willing feet,
May ours be willing too.
So may we grow more like you
In all we say and do.

Or Prayer 2:

Dear heavenly Father, sometimes I feel happy, sometimes I feel sad or angry. I know that it's all right to have these feelings, Lord, but sometimes it makes me feel horrible. Forgive me if I say or do something that's not very nice and help me to become a better friend and person.

Hymn: 'Make me a channel of your peace' (C & P 147)

3 WHAT AM I WORTH?

This is based on the popular TV programme, *The Antiques Roadshow*.

Resources A number of items from your home which vary in price and sentiment, and a blank card for each. Some lard or fat on a plate; some sugar and salt; a few bits of metal; several buckets of water. A box with a lid, with a mirror on the inside.

The items and blank cards are displayed at the front where all can see them.

Leader: Hold up each item in turn, and ask what it is worth. Put the value on the card. When this is completed go through them but make sure there are one or two that are priceless to you but could be worth very little in monetary value; perhaps they are high in sentiment, e.g. the first picture drawn by your child, a vase from Grandma, etc. Point these out to the children and discuss why they are invaluable to you.

Leader: As people, if we looked at how much we are actually worth in money, it wouldn't be very much.

A human body is made up of: a few dollops of fat and a spoonful of sugar. A little bit of metal and salt, and buckets and buckets of water (*these items could be shown*).

But we are very valuable to our parents, brothers, sisters, relations and friends and especially to God. Jesus told us that if God cares about all the birds in the sky and makes beautiful flowers, then how much more he cares for and looks after us.

End by asking for a volunteer who would like to come and have a look at something that is highly precious and unique in the world, but they mustn't tell anyone else.

Have a covered box with a mirror stuck on the inside so that they see themselves when they look in. This can be passed around the class later.

Prayer

Dear Lord, you made this beautiful world with so many different things in it and you care for it all, including us. Thank you for our families, our friends and our school and especially for your love for each one of us.

Song: 'I love the sun' (SSL 12)

14.3 PEOPLE WHO HELP US (OUTLINE)

Aim To involve the children and members of the community, and to show how we depend upon each other. The theme has three parts:

1   People who help us in everyday life.

2   People who help us in school.

3   How we ourselves help people in everyday life and school.

Children were encouraged to make up their own closing prayers, which were shared with the group. During the following weeks many children were writing their own prayers and bringing them to the teacher to read.

2 People who help us in school

An extension of the first topic with many more ideas, possibly due to the fact that the children had had a week to think about people who help us. During this act of worship the local clergyman talked to the children about his work and how he helped people in the community.

Closing prayers were again made up by the children. This led to several more acts of worship on the same theme, including discussions of who helps us and short talks by parents who helped in school. The manager of a residential nursing home near to the school visited and spoke about her work. Dinner supervisors were asked to talk to the children on their role in school, and the Head spoke on her role and duties.

Each act of worship concluded with the children's own prayers.

When this theme was followed in the school which submitted the idea, it developed and lasted for half a term. What made it so special were the 'spin offs' which emerged, which initially had not been planned. These really emerged from part 3, as the children could relate to helping each other. The children became motivated to help, care, be kind, share etc., and enjoyed sharing their experiences with the rest of the school. For the rest of the year, the school enjoyed very special 'Good Deed' assemblies once every three weeks, which the children expected and would discuss prior to the assembly. These 'good deeds' could take place in or out of school and they were shared in an open forum. A reversal had taken place from 'people who help us' to 'us helping others'.

1 People who help us in everyday life

Children were encouraged to give their own ideas about who they thought helped them in their everyday lives. Some good ideas were put forward, such as doctors, dentists, policemen, teachers, vicars and even parents. From this followed good discussion and many of the children's own experiences with these people were talked about. Although this was originally intended to be one act of worship, in practice it was extended to the following week.

3 How we ourselves help other people

Discussions with children following the previous acts of worship led to the preparation of two acts of worship in which some of the children spoke about how they helped others. Their enthusiasm, willingness to share, and kindness and consideration to others were spoken about simply and openly, and it was these two acts of worship that led to the 'Good Deed' assemblies referred to in the introduction.

15 Improvising drama

There is a great big mystique about drama, probably due to all those arty pages in the Sunday papers and all that incomprehensible Shakespeare we were made to read at school. Drama is not, in fact, difficult, obscure and highbrow. Oh, the clever stuff is, yes, the Pinters and suchlike; but at the basic level, it's dead simple, it's 'let's pretend'. We adults, generally, are not very good at it, because we're too self-conscious. But younger children are not self-conscious at all and love playing 'let's pretend'. 'Let's pretend I'm a dragon and I'm coming to eat you up – grr!' Build on that and you've got the basis for an improvised version of St George and the dragon.

Drama in collective worship really doesn't need to be rehearsed at all. Take a good powerful story, like the creation myth of Narreau the Elder from the Polynesian islands, tell the story simply in your own words, and as you go along, pick children to play-act the various characters, and bingo – an instant drama, which the children involved will have loved performing and – more important – which the children watching will remember. It's an unpalatable fact, which those of us who lead acts of worship with children do well to remember, that however good we are at storytelling, leading prayer and accompanying songs on the guitar, children concentrate far more on

what their peers are doing and saying, and are much more likely to get the point and remember it if other children present it to them in dramatic and visual form.

If you do want to polish it up a little, the improvisation could take place in the classroom the day before, and the performance in the act of worship the next morning could use the same children and perhaps minimal costume and props – masks work well and the children enjoy making them. But be prepared for the second run-through to lack something of the sparkle of the first!

The second example here uses simple everyday props, and the narrator describes simple actions which children will have no difficulty in miming.

The third example is so simple it hardly justifies the use of the word drama; but it is offered as an example of something that Key Stage 1 children can do in front of the whole school. And just as children love watching their 'peers' perform, they can often take a genuine, almost paternal interest in what the little ones do.

A few cautionary words:

- If you are involving the children in acting out a story, do tell the story in your own words if you can.

- Do look for ways in which the main body of children can be involved, even if only in standing, sitting, clapping, shouting out, etc. The old pantomime line – 'He's behind you!' – has worked for centuries.

- Do pick children you can rely on to throw themselves into a part without giggling to their friends.

- Don't leave children standing for a long period of time in an uncomfortable posture, e.g. with their hands up 'being a tree'.

- If the drama has been particularly exciting, do calm the children down before sending them back to their classes. Better still, have the worship just before morning playtime.

15.1 NARREAU THE ELDER

Background for the teacher The Polynesian islands in the Pacific Ocean are the home of an ancient people with rich and varied religious traditions. The huge and mysterious stone heads of Easter Island are believed to be statues of gods, but little is known about them or the purpose they served. This story of Narreau the Elder is a creation myth from the Gilbert and Ellis Islands.

Setting This story lends itself to telling 'in the round', all the action taking place in the central space. Two chairs, facing each other, on opposite sides of the stage. A low stage block in the centre.

Pick one child to be Narreau the Elder; tell him to come out and sit on one of the chairs when his name is mentioned.

Narrator: Before anything was, there was Narreau the Elder. Nothing came before him; there was no animal, no fish, no bird, no man before Narreau the Elder. All around him was darkness and emptiness. There was no food, and Narreau neither ate nor felt hunger. There was no night and day, so Narreau did not sleep. For timeless ages, Narreau sat alone in the darkness.

Pick another child to be Narreau the Younger, and tell him/her to be ready to come out and sit on the other chair.

Narrator: Gradually, almost imperceptibly, Narreau began to change. You could not have picked out a single moment in time at which the change happened. But now, instead of being one, he was two: Narreau the Elder and Narreau the Younger. The two gazed steadily at each other, until Narreau the Elder stood up. (*Narreau the Elder stands*) 'My work is nearly finished,' he said. 'All my knowledge and power is yours. There is one thing left for me to do; I will make a universe, upon which you shall practise your skills.' So saying, Narreau the Elder stretched out a hand and created the universe. Then he slowly disappeared, like mists before the morning sun.

Narreau the Elder moves away and sits down at the side. By now, the children playing the parts will have picked up what you want them to do, and will either do it in response to the text, or to a simple gesture from the narrator.

Narrator: Narreau the Younger looked down at the universe that had been created. The earth and sea and sky were still fastened firmly together; they had not yet been separated. Thoughtfully, Narreau walked over the sky, looking for a way through; a crack, a crevice, any way to reach the land below. But there was none.

Narreau knelt down upon the top of the sky. 'I shall use my magical powers,' he said. 'Did not the Elder say that all his knowledge and power was mine? And did he not create this universe for me? I shall take what is mine.'

He stretched out his hand and tapped gently on the surface of the sky. (*Indicate to Narreau the Younger to tap on the stage block.*) Nothing happened. Narreau tapped again. At the third tap, the sky opened. Now Narreau could enter his universe.

From now on, Narreau the Younger will probably pick up the cues from the text.

Narrator: He stood up and looked through the hole in the sky. All was pitch black, and he could see nothing. So he reached out both hands and rubbed his fingertips together. There was a flash of light, and a little luminous moth appeared – the first creature.

The next bit causes adults to giggle – but children's imagination knows no bounds.

Narrator: Narreau smiled and held out his hand. The moth fluttered down and rested on his palm. 'With the light from your body, you can see through the darkness,' Narreau said. 'Go through this opening and tell me what you can see there.' The moth flew down from the sky and disappeared from view.

Indicate to the moth to 'fly' round the room, and come back to Narreau.

Narrator: Some time later he returned, and again settled on the palm of Narreau's hand. 'There are people there, great Narreau,' said the moth. 'But because of the darkness, they are not moving – they are all asleep.'

'I shall see for myself,' announced Narreau. 'Lead the way, little moth, that I may see by your light.'

Indicate to moth and Narreau to go up on to the stage block.

Narrator: By the flickering light of the moth's luminous body, Narreau the Younger found his way to a low mound on the earth, in the middle of all the people. He stretched out his arms so that his fingertips brushed the sky. 'My people!' he cried out in a voice of thunder. 'I am Narreau, your Lord and Creator. I command you – move!'

Indicate to all the children to start to sway.

Narrator: At this, the sleeping bodies began to stir. 'Move, I say!' cried Narreau. 'Stand up, and lift the sky!'

Indicate to the children to stand up and rub their eyes.

Narrator: The people began to stand, and the sky was lifted a little. Light began to appear, and the people blinked and rubbed their eyes. 'Higher!' called Narreau urgently. 'Help me to part the earth and sky!'

Gesture to the children to push upwards as if trying to lift the ceiling.

Narrator: The people pushed upwards, but the sky would not move any further. Narreau realized that the sky was still firmly rooted to the land, and he ordered them to rest. He looked around, and then called Octopus from his hiding place in the sea.

Pick a child to be Octopus. He'll realize what to do.

Narrator: Octopus slithered his way across the land, and flopped down in front of Narreau. 'What is your command, O Master?' he wheezed.

'Return to the sea, Octopus, and fetch Conger Eel from the depths. Tell him I have a task for him that will make him great for ever.'

Whisper to Octopus to go and pick another child to be Conger Eel.

Narrator: Conger Eel, the mighty Lord of the deep sea, could not resist this appeal to his vanity. There was a great surge of foam, and he appeared. His great body curled; he waited for Narreau to speak.

Conger Eel should be curled up in front of Narreau.

Narrator: 'Greetings, Lord of the Depths,' said Narreau. 'Reach up with your mighty body, lift up the sky with your head, and press down the land with your tail. The time has come for the sky and the land to be separated.'

Indicate to Conger Eel to stand up on the stage block and push upwards, as if holding up the ceiling.

Narrator: Eel uncoiled his huge body and pressed up against the sky. Slowly, the great roof of the sky moved upwards as its roots were torn out of the land. The land sank and more light appeared. Narreau looked up; the sky was far enough above the land, but there were no sides to it. 'I shall pull down the sides of the sky, and complete my world,' Narreau said.

Encourage Narreau to run round the edge of the hall, leaping up as if to pull down curtains all round.

Narrator: Leaping up, he caught hold of the edge of the sky and pulled it down to the land, while Eel kept the centre supported on his powerful body. Narreau leapt again and again, pulling down the edges of the sky until it was securely fastened all round and the sky was shaped like a bowl. A shadow fell across the land, and Narreau the Elder reappeared.

Indicate to Narreau the Elder to come on stage again.

Narrator: Narreau the Younger leapt again and with one thrust of his magical sword his father lay dead. Narreau the Younger took his father's right eye and flung it into the sky to the East. It curved through the sky, lighting up the world with dazzling brightness; it was the sun. Narreau took his father's left eye, and flung it West. It was the moon. Narreau took the fragments of his father's shattered body and threw them into the sky, where they became the stars.

Narreau should have no difficulty following these cues; but do watch out in case he starts taking the instructions too literally!

Narrator: Turning to the land, Narreau planted a tree from which grew men; the ancestors of people today. They were the kings of the tree of Samoa, the red-skinned people with the blue eyes.

At last Narreau's work was complete. He looked at his creation, the work of his hands, and as he looked the sun began his journey across the sky. The light grew, and the outline of Narreau the Younger's body slowly became misty and vanished, as his father's had done before. Narreau was never seen again.

Narreau moves slowly to the wings. After a pause, there will usually be spontaneous applause! The narrator can bring the actors forward to take a bow.

Song: 'The bell of creation' (C & P 86)

Reflective prayer

Oh God, we know the world is wonderful but we cannot know exactly how it was made. Thank you for the poets and storytellers who made up the myths and stories of creation, and for the scientists and mathematicians who help us to look back

to the first few seconds of the existence of the universe. Help us to appreciate your love, which brought us into life, and to respond to it by loving others. Amen.

(This version of the act of worship requires no rehearsal. An alternative approach would be to give each actor the lines to speak, and rehearse it the day before.)

The story of Narreau the Elder is taken from *Gods and Men* by Bailey, McLeish and Spearman (OUP).

15.2 CARING FOR THE ENVIRONMENT

Resources Have ready a picnic box with a small table cloth, some cups, crisp bags, can, etc., inside. Have the Country Code on overhead projector.

Before the children enter, scatter rubbish (mainly paper) over the floor. Have the children come in and sit down as normal.

Ask the children what they think of sitting amongst all this rubbish. Do they prefer a clean room? What would happen if everyone dropped rubbish and no one cleared it up? Who should clear it up?

Story/Role play

Tell the story of two families. Two groups of children mime the story as you tell it.

Family A

- Came for a picnic
- Carefully shut the gate behind them
- Looked at the flowers – didn't pick any
- Had their picnic
- Carefully put litter away to take home
- Played quiet games – didn't frighten the animals
- Kept their dog on a lead
- Left everything as they found it.

Family B

- Came for a picnic
- Left the gate open
- Picked flowers
- Had their picnic
- Threw the litter away
- Played noisy games – frightened animals
- Didn't keep dog under control
- Left behind a mess!

Ask what would happen if we all behaved like Family B (no wild flowers, litter, like on the floor today, pollution). How should we behave?

Remind the children of the Country Code (on overhead projector):

1 Close gates behind you.
2 Keep off the crops.
3 Don't frighten the animals.
4 Take your litter home.
5 Leave things as you find them.

Prayer

Thank you, God, for the countryside and for all living things. Help us to look after the places where we live. Help us to remember to throw our rubbish away in the proper place. Help us to care for our environment. Amen.

Song: 'Milk bottle tops and paper bags' (SSL 17)

Ending: Ask for volunteers to clean up the room!

15.3 SHARING

This would be appropriate for Harvest Festival or Christian Aid Week. The children doing the acting could be Key Stage 1 children.

Resources Some books, coloured pencils and pens, rubbers, maths equipment. Table at front. One small sweet. Large piece of card, or OHP slide, with the word 'SHARING'.

Introductory music: 'Food glorious food' (from *Oliver*).

Leader: Today we're going to think about the word 'sharing'. (*Display card or OHP*)

We all know what that means, don't we? It's easy – at least it is when we've enough to share. Look at (*names of children*) sharing things out ready for a lesson.

Group of children come forward. One carries books, one pencils and pens, one rubbers, one some pieces of maths equipment. One child sorts them out and allocates them so that each has a book, a pencil, a rubber, and an item of equipment. They sit down at the front.

Leader: But when there isn't enough to go round, it's much more difficult. (*Holds up a sweet for all to see, and places it on table*) I wonder how the same children would share this one sweet?

The same group of children stand round the table and talk about how they might share it. Offers might include 'chop it up', 'one of us eat it', and 'give it to your friend'.

Leader: It's much more difficult to share when there's not enough to go round, isn't it? There's a story in the Bible when the crowds following Jesus didn't have enough food to go round.

Story

Tell the story of the Feeding of the 5,000 in simple words, as follows:

When the disciples came back after Jesus had sent them out in pairs teaching and healing, they were very tired. Jesus decided that they needed some time to rest, away from the crowds. They went by boat across the lake to find a lonely spot well away from any towns or villages.

Unfortunately, lots of people saw them leave and guessed where they were going. They hurried off round the shore of the lake, gathering other people on the way. By the time Jesus and his disciples arrived in their boat, the shore was crowded with people eagerly waiting for them.

'Oh no!' groaned the disciples. 'There goes our day of peace and quiet!'

'Shall we carry on round the lake, Master?' asked one. 'They might give up and go home.'

'No, we can't do that,' Jesus replied. 'Look at them – they're like sheep without a shepherd. I must go and speak to them.'

They brought the boat ashore and Jesus began to speak to the crowds. The day wore on, but nobody showed any sign of wanting to go home.

In the afternoon the disciples came to Jesus. 'It's getting very late, Master', they said.

'Don't you think we ought to send these people off to get themselves something to eat and drink?'

Jesus was thinking about the talks he was having with the people, not about food. 'Yes, yes,' he said. 'You organize it.'

'You mean we have to buy food for all these thousands of people?' the disciples protested.

'How much food do you have?' Jesus asked.

The disciples went to have a look.

'We have five loaves of bread, and we caught two fish in the lake this morning,' they said.

'Ask the people to sit down on the grass,' Jesus said.

Everyone sat down and Jesus took the bread and the fish and said the blessing. Then he gave the food to his disciples to give out to the people. There must have been five thousand people there, but somehow, despite the small amount of food, suddenly everyone seemed to have something to eat.

Reflection

Discuss with the children what might have happened. Draw out the possibility that one person had offered to share his loaves and fish, and gradually others had done the same.

If the context is Harvest Festival, explain that what we are doing when we bring samples of the harvest of food to church is to offer them to God, then to share them with those in need. If the context is Christian Aid Week, talk about how we might share out the world's food resources more fairly.

Song: 'When I needed a neighbour' (C & P 65)

Prayer

We thank you, God, for all the food we have to eat, and for the people who provide for us. Help us to remember those who are less well off than ourselves, and to think of ways in which we can share what we have with others. Amen.

16 Getting into dialogue

Using question-and-answer techniques is a familiar part of the teacher's armoury which works well in a class of 30, especially when the teacher knows all the children well and can gently encourage those less willing to have a go, and equally gently suppress the exuberant. It's much more difficult with a school hall full of four- to eleven-year-olds, especially when you don't know all their names. The infants put their hands up for everything, but generally just want to tell you what they had for breakfast, and there's always one or two quietly confident older ones who probably go to Sunday school and know the Bible better than you do.

It's even more difficult when you have 500 children in a church with poor acoustics and the visiting preacher insists on asking questions, but no one, least of all the speaker at the front, can hear the answers!

Nevertheless, the technique is an invaluable part of getting, and keeping, the children involved. There are lots of examples, throughout the book, of ways of involving children in dialogue; the two acts of worship in this chapter just happen to rely heavily on this technique.

A few caveats, with apologies for teaching my grandmother to suck eggs:

- Do have a broad idea of where you want the dialogue to go, and don't be afraid to steer it in that direction.

- Do acknowledge every answer, even if it's quite different from what you wanted or expected! Be encouraging – say things like: 'Now that's really good – I'd never thought of that.' 'Yes I like that, but I was thinking more of...'

- Don't let it go on too long.

- Don't leave the children (usually the infants) with their hands in the air. When you've drawn out what you want, and you're ready to move on, say 'Hands down.'

- Don't let them get too excited. Someone else has to calm them down and teach them their tables.

- Don't forget this is supposed to be worship, not a rehearsal for *Brain of Britain*. A few questions to get everyone's mind working on the theme will be quite enough.

- Don't let the same child answer every question, even if she is the vicar's daughter.

16.1 COMMUNITY (IN PREPARATION FOR HARVEST FESTIVAL LATER IN THE WEEK)

Aim To encourage children to prepare for Harvest Festival as a time to say 'thank you' to others, and to encourage a 'Family of Christ' feeling.

Resources The school had borrowed a harvest sheaf from the baker, who bakes one annually for the parish church, and this and a piece of vine grown in the garden of a villager provided the visual focus. Behind the table with these objects was a display which is used as a focus for collective worship. This board had been freshly changed to show three posters from Christian Aid of people

around the world using their hands to make/cultivate food, e.g. bread, vegetables. Around the pictures were cut-out shapes of hands of different size and colour.

Entry music: Pastoral Symphony (Beethoven)

Hymn: 'Lord of the harvest' (C & P 133) or any other harvest hymn.

Leader: After introducing the objects and the display, ask the children to reflect on the message, the link between them and any response they may like to share. These are some ideas they may come up with:

- Hands are tools to use the world's resource.

- By sharing there is enough for all.

- We can use our hands to give as well as make (i.e. charity and donations).

- Bread was used by Jesus as a symbol of basic food which all people need.

- A vine was used by Jesus as a symbol of himself working through and with his disciples.

- Bread and wine are symbols of celebrating and special occasions.

- Bread and wine are symbols of belonging to the church family because they are shared together at the Eucharist service.

These ideas could be put up on flip charts and displayed round the hall.

SIXTEEN

Prayer

Use the words of the song 'You are the Vine' (MP 792) with pauses between verses during which the leader of worship reflects on the way in which everyone present is part of the Christian family.

Conclusion

Explain the relevance of the choice of entry and going-out music – the Pastoral Symphony – as part of the Harvest focus.

Going-out music: Pastoral Symphony.

16.2 COURAGE (THE STORY OF ST PATRICK, FOR ST PATRICK'S DAY)

Age range: Key Stage 1

Entry music: Irish folk music.

Introduction

Introduce the fact that it is St Patrick's Day. Explain that one of the reasons we remember St Patrick is because of his courage. Ask the children to share any recent experiences they have had of being brave.

(Responses may include visit to doctor or dentist, or a stay in hospital; leaving parents for first time, e.g. first day in school; going on a train or on the underground; losing sight of Mum in the supermarket. Remember these are very young children!)

Story

Tell the story of St Patrick and the Christian fire. (Kidnapped by pirates and taken to Ireland; made to look after pigs; escaped to a boat, but found himself in France; sought refuge in a monastery; trained to be a priest and felt called to go to Ireland; landed in Ireland and lit a fire, to the fury of the locals who said it was Druid law that only the Druid king could light a fire at the time of the Spring festival; Patrick defies the Druid king and tells him about Jesus; Druid king is baptized.)

A full version of the story may be found in *Red Letter Days* by Jeanne Jackson (Stanley Thornes, 1995).

Reflective prayer

Make an improvised prayer based on the examples children gave of the times they have had to be brave, relating this to Patrick's courage and asking God's grace and strength to continue to be brave to stand up for what we believe, as Patrick did.

Song: 'Magic penny' (A 10)

Going-out music: Irish folk tunes.

17 Using artefacts

Artefacts of various kinds can be very useful as audio-visual aids when talking to children in worship. Religious artefacts are increasingly used in religious education to help children to understand key ideas in religion, and many schools will have a 'Jewish box' with Seder plate, tephillin, menorah, prayer shawl, etc.; a 'Sikh box' with the five Ks of Sikhism; and so on. These will, of course, mainly be used in class, but there will be occasions when it is appropriate to use them in collective worship – an enactment of a

Seder meal at Passover time, for example (see 9.3), or in telling the story of Judah Maccabee at Hanukkah.

Other, secular, artefacts can provide the central focus for a talk in the act of worship; the examples given here are a sewing machine and cotton, to illustrate the point that strong components and weak components work together to make an end product; hand tools, ranging from stone age implements to the latest DIY technology, to illustrate the way in which human beings

shape their environment; candles, for a series of acts of worship on the theme of light.

Finally, attention must be drawn to the desirability of using artefacts, both religious and secular, as a focus for worship every day. Most school worship takes place in a multi-purpose school hall, with wall bars and other PE equipment, lighting bars for drama purposes, sometimes with music stands and musical instruments. For a few short minutes every day, this hive of educational busyness has to become a shrine, a hallowed place, a place set aside for the worship of God. This is not an easy transformation to make, but artefacts can help. A table at the front, with a plain white tablecloth and a vase of fresh flowers, provides a simple, dramatic and non-denominational focus for any kind of theme. Many schools have a cross or crucifix prominently on display, either permanently or during worship. A candle, prominently placed at the front, can be lit to indicate the beginning of worship and blown out at the end. Some schools have a backdrop of large-scale work by pupils, both two- and three-dimensional, on the theme for the week. Some have a motto or text on display for a period of time.

A word of caution: don't overdo it! Too many artefacts, symbols, pictures, candles and displays of work can be confusing and distracting. Keep it simple.

17.1 WORKING TOGETHER

Age range: Key Stage 2

Resources Key objects: Sewing machine, cotton reel with ordinary cotton.

Introductory music: 'Help' (The Beatles)

Introduction

Talk about how we work together in school. The teaching staff, both teachers and ancillaries, work as a team, planning, preparing and delivering the lessons.

Ask the children questions to draw out how they work together in school.

(Responses may include working in groups in technology projects; team games; playing together in band and recorder group.)

Ask what problems we encounter when we work with others.

(Answers may include disagreements, selfishness, taking over, not listening to each other, etc.)

Hymn: 'Lord of all hopefulness' (C & P 52)

Draw attention to key objects – sewing machine and cotton reel with ordinary cotton. Ask pupils to look at the sewing machine and volunteer words that describe it: e.g. strong, made of iron, heavy, powerful.

Ask pupils to look at the cotton on the reel and describe this. Snap the thread for greater effect. Words to look for are light, weak, thin, etc. These can be matched against each one on the sewing machine list.

A flip chart or blackboard could be used to list the words – one column for the sewing machine, one for the cotton.

Ask pupils what a sewing machine does and go on to explain that on its own it has no use until a reel of cotton is added.

Key idea

Only by working together can the sewing machine complete the job required. Strong

works with weak and each becomes equally important. (For further effect, an electric sewing machine can be used and the invisible power of electricity likened to the invisible power of God.)

Conclusion

Summarize by reminding children that Jesus called together a band of very ordinary people to work with him and carry on his work after his death – fishermen, a customs officer, a member of the resistance movement. None of them were priests, or members of the official religious groups of the time such as Pharisees or Sadducees. They all had their strengths and weaknesses, and by working together and trusting in the power of God in their lives (the electricity in the machine) they became a powerful force that transformed the world.

Prayer

> Dear Lord, help all people strong and weak, old and young, to work together. Help us to learn to live as members of society; to be able to share things, to bear things and be tolerant of all people we work with. Amen.

Closing hymn: 'When I needed a neighbour' (C & P 65)

17.2 PAST, PRESENT AND FUTURE

An act of worship which helps children form a perspective on the way in which society has changed and evolved and to look forward to the future, and emphasizes that they are all potentially important in the future development of mankind.

Resources Three cards, with the words PAST, PRESENT and FUTURE, placed on three tables at the front. Key objects: A range of hand tools, going back to primitive stone-age hammers and flints (copies, made by older children, or pictures could be used). Old hammers, saws, etc. can be acquired from parents and friends of the school. Modern, state of the art DIY equipment, depending on the school's contacts; a local firm may help.

Age range: Key Stage 2

Introductory music: Theme from *Star Wars*.

Song: 'He's got the whole world in his hand' (C & P 19)

Introduction

Talk briefly about each object without giving its age. Ask children what each object is and what it is used for. Jumble them up and ask the children to say which table they should go on – Past, Present or Future. (When this is finished, there should of course not be any objects on the 'Future' table. Ask the children why this is.)

Key idea

What of the future? Explain to the children that they will play an important part in the future of our world. What sort of world will that be? If you follow the example of Jesus and try to be kind, thoughtful and good it is possible that our world will be a happy and safe place to live in. We cannot change the past or what has happened to these objects but we can affect the future.

Symbolic action

Take a child and sit him/her on the 'Future' table. Children are the future; the tools, implements and artefacts of the future are in their minds. Discuss this with the children.

Prayer

> Dear God, help us to remember things that happened long ago. Some things were bad, some were good. Let us work together as friends to make the future world a better place for all. Amen.

Closing hymn: 'God who made the earth' (C & P 10)

- genuine antique candlestick
- candle used at a baptism
- candles used on a church altar
- small candles used for personal prayer
- a Paschal candle
- an Advent ring, with four red candles and one white one.

Setting School hall, curtains closed and no lights on. (Very atmospheric!)

The children sit in a horse-shoe formation, facing the front, where there is a cross on the wall and a table with an unlit candle in a candlestick on it (see below).

Entry music: As the children arrive for assembly, they join in singing several choruses (C & P).

Introduction

Following the customary 'Good morning', the children are quiet.

Leader lights the candle, with no comment. Pause.

Leader: (*Quietly*) Can you all see the candle?

Response: Yes.

17.3 CANDLES

This act of worship was the first in a series which lasted about three weeks, beginning just before Advent. Other acts of worship during this period included those taken by visiting clergy, and praise and worship style assemblies.

Resources For each act of worship, appropriate artefacts were brought in and used. They included:

Leader: It's a very small candle – are you sure?

Response: Yes.

Leader: Our hall is very large – can those of you at the back see the candle?

Response: Yes.

Leader: Isn't it strange how one small candle can be seen everywhere in a large, gloomy hall? Hmmmmm (*Pause for reflective silence*)

Development of theme

Leader: (*Change of tempo and voice*) How many of you use candles at home, to light the rooms?

Response: Nil.

Leader: Well then – what do you use instead?

Responses will include lights, lamps, etc.

Leader: (*Summarizing*) That's right – we usually use electric lights of some kind, don't we? (*Pause*) We will use candles at home sometimes. Can you think when we might use them?

Responses will include birthday cakes, Christmas decorations, special meals, when the electricity is cut off, etc.

Leader: A long time ago, before people had electricity in their homes, they didn't have lights like we do. When my mother was a little girl, she didn't have electricity. She only had candles in her home. Candles were very precious, and also a bit dangerous, so she had to look after them properly. This is a candlestick that my mother used when she was a little girl. She used to take it up to her bedroom at night and then, when she was ready to go to sleep, she would blow it out. (*Genuine artefact shown to the children*)

Prayer

Dear Lord, thank you for the lights in our homes. They help us to see, they help us to play, and they help us to work. They also help us not to be frightened in the dark. Amen.

Song: 'This little light of mine' (A 14)

Conclusion

The children leave the hall in silence, watching the candle burning until it is their turn to leave.

Later acts of worship in the series developed the idea of children being 'lights' in peoples' lives, bringing joy, love and friendship to others, just like a candle shining in the darkness. This then led to the theme of 'Jesus Christ, the light of the world'.

17.4 COMMUNITY

This assembly deals with something that children come into contact with each day – sheets of paper!

It's about the strength gained from acting together; about unity of purpose and how we expect all members of our school community to work for the good of all.

Resources Cards with key words – unity, unison, etc. Ream of A4 paper, some different kinds of paper, e.g. tissue.

Introductory music: 'Paper moon'.

Introduce words such as unity, unison, co-operation, agreement, harmony, etc. Have these on cards to hold up and focus on.

Talk about the pleasure we get from our school working together; the satisfaction gained from group or class projects; about the pride of representing the school at netball or football, or some other team game. Go on to talk about the hurt felt when individuals or groups let the school or friends down. Recent examples of these could be found from the day-to-day life of the school.

To reinforce this, have several children 'primed', each with a sheet of A4 paper. Ask them to bring these out one at a time. Take each sheet and tear it, showing how easy this is (you could ask each child to do this). Have on the desk an open ream of A4 paper (or a large number of sheets – e.g. one sheet for each person in the school!). Then show how hard it is to tear apart – if enough sheets are used, it can be made impossible.

The moral of this exposition can be drawn from children, that by acting collectively, supporting others, and pursuing common aims we can create strong bonds between us.

Song: 'Black and white' (C & P 67) or 'The family of man' (C & P 69)

Prayer

Help us, Almighty Father, to see the world as you made it – a world where everyone and everything has its place. Give us your gift of love so that we may realize that all the world is our neighbour, and we are all equally important members of your great family. Amen.

Index of themes

Together with Children

Together with Children provides practical, topical resource material and information about wider issues in church and school children's work. Its regular features are a real source of inspiration for leaders.

Regular Features:

◆ a complete all-age service

◆ stories

◆ sketches

◆ activities for special days and festivals

◆ articles by colleagues in the field of children's work

◆ reviews of key new resources and books

◆ a topical feature on a current issue for children's leaders

If you work with the under 12s, we're certain that you'll like it.

Call 0171 898 1499 today to receive your free sample copy.

Together with Children (£1.80 per issue) is published nine times a year and is available from all good Christian bookshops (ISSN 1361-1429), or by subscription. For more details please phone Marie Yateman on 0171 898 1499.

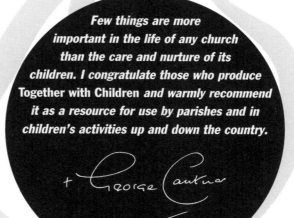

Few things are more important in the life of any church than the care and nurture of its children. I congratulate those who produce **Together with Children** *and warmly recommend it as a resource for use by parishes and in children's activities up and down the country.*

+ George Cantuar

ARCHBISHOP OF CANTERBURY

THE NATIONAL SOCIETY
LEADING EDUCATION WITH A CHRISTIAN PURPOSE
REG CHARITY NO. 313070

THE NATIONAL SOCIETY

Searching for a sketch for a school assembly or family service?

Look no further than The National Society and Church House Publishing's best-selling drama

Playing Up
Dave Hopwood

Over 30 witty and thought-provoking sketches
£6.95

0 7151 4895 8

Acting Up
Dave Hopwood

- Raps
- mimes
- monologues

£5.95

0 7151 4866 4

Plays on the Word
Derek Haylock

Nineteen fast-moving, Bible-based sketches, including eight for Christmas
£5.95

0 7151 4824 9

Plays for all Seasons
Derek Haylock

A collection of 21 dramas and plays covering the whole Christian year
£6.95

0 7151 4884 2

A Fistful of Sketches
Dave Hopwood

Sketches • raps • prayers • performance poems. Ideal for the older members of the youth group
£5.95

0 7151 4869 9

All titles above are available from your local Christian bookshop.

The National Society (Church of England) for Promoting Religious Education supports everyone involved in Christian education – teachers, school governors, students, parents, clergy, parish and diocesan education teams – with its legal and professional advice, the resources of its RE centres, courses, conferences and archives.

It is a voluntary Anglican society, also operating ecumenically, and helps to promote inter-faith education and dialogue through its RE centres.

For more details of the Society, or a copy of our current resources catalogue or details on how you can support the continuing work of the Society, please call 0171-898 1499 or email: info@natsoc.c-of-e.org.uk

For more details see our online catalogue: www.chpublishing.co.uk.